White Peak

Dalesman Publishing Company
Stable Courtyard, Broughton Hall,
Skipton, North Yorkshire BD23 3AE

First Edition 1997

Text © Martin Smith 1997
Cover: Milldale, Derbyshire by Derek Forss
Maps by Jeremy Ashcroft
Printed by Amadeus Press, Huddersfield

A British Library Cataloguing in Publication
record is available for this book

ISBN 185568 099 8

White Peak

Martin Smith

Series editor Terry Marsh

DALESMAN

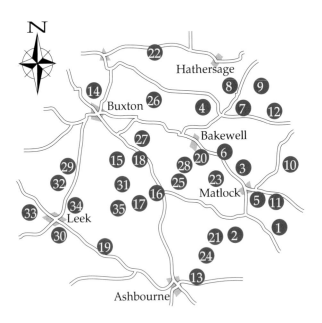

Contents

Introduction

The Peak District is divided into two sections, the Dark Peak to the north, and the White Peak. Strictly, the White Peak is the lower, limestone area, pastoral and deep cut by beautiful dales. However, the limestone only outcrops in the central area of the Peak District National Park and is surrounded by shale and gritstone moors. To the east, it dips beneath the shales and grits, only to re-emerge again at Crich and Ashover. In the heart of the limestone area there are isolated pockets of gritstone scenery, where the overlying rock has not been eroded to the same extent as elsewhere.

Running throughout the limestone, and the source of much of the ancient wealth of the villages of the area, are mineral veins, containing lead, barytes, fluorspar, calcite, etc. The landscape is riddled with mines and quarries, many long since closed and of great industrial archaeological interest, some very obviously modern and operational.

Man's influence on this landscape goes back thousands of years. Virtually every hilltop has its burial mound. Archaeological evidence suggests that the limestone was cleared of trees in pre-historic times and the land has been farmed ever since. Old settlements there are in plenty, some no more than grassy mounds where sheep now graze, others still enjoying a vibrant life.

The limestone scarcely reaches a height of more

than 1,000ft/300m and for the most part it forms a plateau, where the obvious features are the network of drystone walls, the burial mounds and the villages. Appearances are deceptive, however, for often a stroll across the plateau leads to an abrupt drop into a spectacular dale, like Lathkill or Dove.

The area covered

It would have been a fairly easy task to have devised 35 walks that never strayed out of the main limestone area, but I have included the outlying limestone areas of Ashover and Crich and the fringing gritstone, for instance, near the Roaches and on the East Moors, near Chesterfield and Sheffield.

Choice of walks

The walks all start at a place that can be reached by a reasonable public transport service, but most of the walks are circular, so if you are firmly wedded to your car, the use of a bus or train is not compulsory. However, some walks are linear and here you have no choice but to use the bus or train.

Tips for public transport use

Always check the bus/train times beforehand. Contact telephone numbers are given on page 219, but you are advised to purchase a copy of Derbyshire County Council's Peak District public transport timetable, which contains details of all the services in the area covered by this book, and is available from any of the Information Centres. Look out for discount ticket offers, for families, groups or allowing travel on more than one day, or on services provided by more than one operator.

Maps

Most of the walks are contained on the OS Outdoor Leisure map 24: The White Peak. Where this is not the case the relevant 1:25000 Outdoor Leisure or Pathfinder map is indicated. Note: Over the next few years, all the Pathfinder maps will be replaced by the new Explorer series.

Rights of way

The Peak District has a fine network of footpaths and bridleways, most of which are easy to follow. In the area covered by this book, the authorities responsible for their repair and maintenance are Derbyshire and Staffordshire County Councils, with assistance from the district councils, the parishes and the Peak District National Park. Please report any difficulties to one or other of these bodies.

Care of the countryside

Please remember that the countryside is a working environment, someone else's livelihood. You will not endear yourself to the locals by letting dogs or children run riot, by dropping litter, by leaving gates open or damaging stiles and walls. Take nothing but photographs, leave nothing but footprints.

Enjoy your walking.

The Derwent Valley

The Derwent is Derbyshire's river. From its source in the far north of the county, to its confluence with the Trent, it exerts a tremendous influence on the scenic quality, the land form and the economic livelihood of those who dwell near its banks. By the time it reaches the confines of this book, it is a well-established river, running through a deep cut valley. At this stage it has already been dammed three times and its water siphoned off to supply East Midlands towns and Sheffield. Industry has also made its mark, but despite this the river retains its beauty and purity, slipping gently through the wooded valley between Hathersage and Grindle-ford, before resuming its southward course.

Between Grindleford and Baslow the valley is guarded on the east by the frowning walls of the Edges, playgrounds for climbers and walkers alike.

At Baslow the river passes into a totally different landscape where it enters Chatsworth Park. Here the river forms a major feature of the landscaped parkland, beautifully blended with the now well-established trees; a superb setting for the Palace of the Peak, Chatsworth House.

Beyond the Park, the river enters the gritstone and shale landscape of Rowsley and Darley Dale, sharing its valley with housing, industry, railway and roads. Still it is the dominant feature, as it sweeps through these villages and on into the Matlock limestone. Here is water sculpture at its best, a mighty gash in the limestone forming a spectacular gorge, with Masson Hill rising to the west and castle-crowned Riber to the east.

Beyond Cromford the river leaves the limestone again and the valley widens out, sweeping down through fields and woods past Whatstandwell, to join the Amber at Ambergate.

The walks in this section all visit the river at some point, except the Carsington reservoir circuit. This justifies its inclusion by the fact that the vast bulk of the reservoir's waters are drawn from the Derwent, a final example of a process started many miles further north near the source.

1 Ambergate and Crich

A steady climb through the lovely Shining Cliff Woods leads to Alderwasley. Fine views of the Derwent valley follow as the walk descends to Whatstandwell. A stiff pull with compensating views leads to Crich and the subsequent walk along The Tors is a delight.

Distance:
7¼ miles/12km
Height gain:
1,350 ft/ 415m
Walking time:
4 ½ hours
Start/Finish:
Ambergate Station.
GR348526. Parking at
the station.
Type of walk:
A combination of

woodland and field
paths, mostly well
defined, but with steep
sections.
Public transport:
Daily bus and train
services from
Ambergate to Derby
and Matlock. Other
bus services to Ripley
and Alfreton.

Ambergate lies at the confluence of the rivers Derwent and Amber. There are pubs, shops and cafes, a nearby youth hostel, bed and breakfasts and campsites.

From Ambergate Station go left along the A610, turning left at the A6 by the Hurt Arms. At the junction by the church, go right, soon crossing the Derwent. Just over the river, turn right, paralleling the mill leat for about 220yds/m before climbing to a

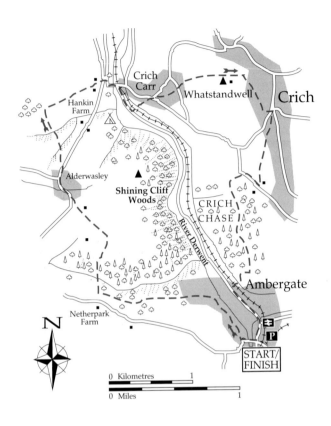

junction of tracks and paths. Just beyond, at another fork, keep left, passing houses and entering Beggarswell Wood. The track rises through the wood, passing a number of isolated properties. After the final bungalow a broad path leads deeper into the wood. Bear right where the track forks, descending into the valley of Peat Pits Brook. At the lake keep left, through delightful woodland, gradually climbing, beside a stream. The path steepens appreciably before skirting the rocky head of a small side stream, close to Netherbank Farm, where it reaches a track. Bear right.

A culvert carries the track across the brook to a junction. Keep left here and in about 100yds/m go right at a waymark, climbing swiftly to the edge of Typeclose Plantation. Pass through a gate and follow a wall and wood on the right. At the end of the wood, the path passes into a walled lane, soon reaching Park Plantation.

Park Plantation forms the southern fringe of Alderwasley Park, but unrestricted grazing by sheep has meant that there is no undergrowth and very little new tree growth at all.

Follow the track by the wall, soon passing the war memorial and reaching the road. Pass the driveway to the church and hall, continuing up the road to a T-junction. Go straight on, before turning left at a stile, opposite the entrance to Home Farm.

Go down to the bottom left corner of the field, then right, to a gate and stile, turning left alongside a hedge. Cross a stream before climbing the next field to a junction of paths. Turn right and begin the descent to the Derwent.

Go straight ahead through fields to Hilltop Farm. Pass to the right of the farm buildings, along a narrow lane, and then on a path to the right of the farm access. The path crosses the access and continues on the opposite side, descending very steeply before turning sharp right, to reach the road near Whatstandwell Bridge. Cross the bridge and at the junction just beyond the Derwent Hotel, ascend the minor road, signed to Crich, soon crossing the railway line and Cromford Canal.

The original 1848 Whatstandwell station can be seen to the left. It closed in 1894, being replaced by a new "more commodious" station on the opposite side of the bridge.

About 220yds/m beyond the bridge, bear left up Hindersitch Lane, climbing steeply and soon swinging left by an old chapel. After a further 110yds/m, bear right at the junction, continuing uphill until the road finishes. A narrow ginnel leads alongside The Willows to another road. Go right here for a short distance, before turning left up a signposted ginnel between houses. A flight of steps leads steeply up, crossing an overgrown lane and a farm track, climbing a few more steps, into fields where the gradient eases and Crich Stand can be seen just to the left.

Go straight on through fields with the spire of Crich church soon coming into view, forming a useful marker. When the top of the hill is reached, the path still heads for Crich church. Go right on reaching a track, which emerges into a narrow lane. Follow the lane, soon passing a fine stone bridge.

The bridge used to carry the Crich Mineral Railway en route from the quarry near the Stand to the Midland Railway at Ambergate. Built by Stephenson in the 1840s, this line enjoyed over a hundred years of life before the closure of the quarry removed its reason for existence.

Continue along the road past housing, before turning left at a T-junction to reach Crich Square. In the Square, turn right, up Sandy Lane, by the chapel. Beyond the reading rooms on the left, take a path on top of the grassy bank, before passing through a stile to the left of a bungalow.

Soon there is a tremendous view both right and left. To the left Bolsover Castle and Hardwick Hall can be seen on top of the magnesian limestone ridge. To the right the scene stretches into the heart of the limestone Peak.

Stroll along the top of The Tors, former gritstone quarry workings. To the right the land slopes steeply away to the Derwent valley. There are few places in Derbyshire where one gets an impression of being on a ridge top, but here is one of them. The path soon descends to the road at Chadwick Nick. Here the road cuts through the ridge in a pronounced V. Turn right, following the road to a right-hand bend.

Go left here, following a wall to the bottom of the field. Go left again, on a path along the edge of the valley, soon entering Crich Chase Wood, a delightful area of mixed deciduous woodland. An obvious path twists and turns through the trees to a more open area, with a ruined barn on the left.

The path begins to descend to the right, passing through a gateway and into more woodland. Where the path forks, bear left, descending to join another track. Almost at once, bear right, down a narrow, twisting hollow way. On reaching open fields, go right, down to a gate in the far left-hand corner. Pass through the gate, over the canal and the railway to reach the A6. Follow the main road to the left for about 500yds/m to the junction by the Hurt Arms, then left to Ambergate station.

2 Carsington Water

This walk can be made very easy by omitting the stretch between Wirksworth and Carsington, but that would lessen the sense of achievement. The hardest climbing is the ascent from Wirksworth. The circuit of Carsington Water is very well waymarked.

Distance:
10³/₄ miles/17km
Height gain:
1,650ft/ 550m
Walking time:
6¹/₄ hours
Start/Finish:
Wirksworth Market Place. GR286530. Parking in town centre.
Type of walk:
Generally an easy walk
on well waymarked paths, with the steepest climb at the start.
Public transport:
Wirksworth is served by daily buses from Bakewell, Matlock, Belper and Derby and by a sparse Monday to Saturday service from Ashbourne.

Wirksworth is a fine old market town, of considerable antiquity, certainly having Saxon origins and possibly Roman. The source of the town's wealth was lead and there are some very interesting Saxon carvings depicting leadminers in the parish church. The leadminers' court, the Barmoot, still meets at Wirksworth. The story of the mines and the quarries is told in the heritage centre and at the nearby National Stone Centre.

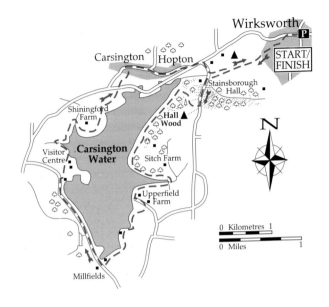

Go up the Ashbourne road, before turning left along Yokecliffe Lane, which soon forks. Go left, descending gently behind new houses. After about 300yds/m, where the lane swings to the right, go left at a stile. A narrow ginnel leads to Yokecliffe Drive. Go right here, for about 200yds/m to a footpath sign on the right. A stone path leads between houses, emerging into fields near a barn.

Follow the path through the first field, through a gateway, then take the left-hand fork. A stile at the edge of the field leads into a sunken lane. Go right, following this lane to the top of the hill, where there are stiles right and left, with good views, reaching to the Dovedale hills. Go left, descending through remains of lead mining to another lane, almost opposite the entrance to Stainsbro' Hall.

Go left again, climbing quite sharply, almost to the top of Soldiers' Knoll. Just after a small plantation, a waymarked path to the right strikes across the brow of the field, before descending to the reservoir perimeter track. Turn left, following the waymarked Carsington circular walk.

The route, much of it wooded, now needs little description, though it does not hug the lake shore as might be expected. Occasionally the path descends almost to the water's edge, rounding a sizeable inlet near Sitch Farm. At Upperfield Farm the route crosses the old road, which now finishes abruptly at the water's edge. Twin routes for walkers and cyclists continue from here. Soon Millfields car park and picnic site are reached, whence the way lies along the crest of the dam, with a view to the left over the village of Hognaston.

The water for this reservoir is not provided by the meagre stream that graces this valley. Instead a complex system of tunnels links the lake to the Derwent valley and water can be pumped in either direction.

Pass the sailing club and the visitor centre, continuing on the waymarked route, signposted Sheepwash, out of the northern end of the car park. A pleasant path round the northern shore soon reaches Sheepwash car park and then the B5035. Cross the road and continue along the waymarked route into Carsington village, close to the pub. Skirt to the left of the pub to reach the old main road. Go right, following the road through Carsington to Hopton. As the road skirts Hopton Hall, note the unusual boundary wall. At the end of the wall there is a blind bend, with very little verge on the right. It is safer to walk on the left here. When the B5035 is rejoined, bear left for a short distance, and at the next junction, go right.

There is a fine stone guide post in the grass triangle, bearing four names, but there are now only three roads. The fourth passed through the farmyard and up the hillside, heading for Bakewell and Buxton.

Go down the lane for a short distance, then turn left up a narrow rough track. Follow this as it climbs steadily, soon bending to the right. At the top of the hill there are stiles right and left and here the outward route is rejoined. Go through the left-hand stile and follow the obvious path through a series of fields, past the Yokecliffe lead mines until the little barn is reached and the path returns to suburbia. Follow the outward route back into Wirksworth.

3 Darley Dale and Sydnope

The walk wanders along the Derwent valley before climbing up to Stancliffe, Northwood and a fine viewpoint at Fallinge Edge. A moorland trek follows, then a fine old coach route, down to Sydnope. Finally there is a delightful stroll through Ladygrove, back to Darley Dale.

Distance: 8½ miles/14km **Height gain:** 960ft/290m **Walking time:** 4 hours **Start/Finish:** Darley Dale Station. GR273625. Car parking at Darley Bridge picnic site. GR270624.	**Type of walk:** Old packhorse routes and some moorland walking on indistinct paths. Easy climbing. **Public transport:** Daily buses to Darley Dale from Nottingham, Derby, Matlock, Bakewell, Buxton, Stockport and Manchester.

From the station, follow the path by the railway to Church Lane level crossing. Go over the level crossing and in 110yds/m turn right, along Abbey House Drive, passing Abbey House on the left. At the stables the road becomes a grassy lane and reaches open fields, with a view across the valley to Stanton Moor and Grey's Tower.

Keep alongside the wall, soon passing a barn.

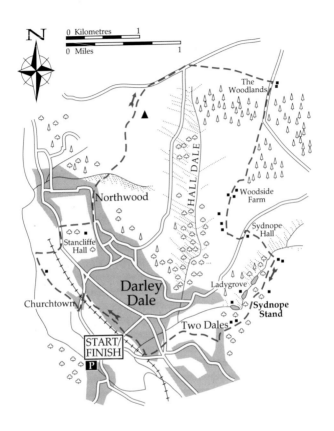

Carry straight on, now with a fence to the left. Go through the gateway on the right and bear right in the next field, soon crossing the railway again. Negotiate a slippery plank bridge over a ditch, then cross the field to the A6. Turn left along the road, crossing as quickly as possible. Pass the first few houses on the right, until a track is reached, just before the bus stop.

Go right, into a field, climbing close to the boundary wall of Stancliffe Quarry Wood, until a lane is reached. Go left here for 435yds/m, to the junction with Lumb Lane, where there is an extensive view to Rowsley and Calton.

Bear right up Lumb Lane, climbing steadily, soon leaving the houses behind, and passing Pax Tor, where the lane becomes a rough track. Follow the track up by the stream keeping right at the fork, then leaving the stream, bearing to the left in a deep cut hollow-way.

A delightful stretch of green lane now follows, walled and narrowed still further by oak, hazel, birch and holly. Continue up onto open moorland, with the trig point of Little Bumper Piece just to the right. The track now levels off for the final approach to the top of Rowsley Bar.

Here is a tremendous view to the left, straight up the Wye valley towards Haddon and Bakewell, and on a clear day the gritstone hills beyond Buxton can be seen. To the right lie Calton Pastures, Chatsworth and the length of the Derwent valley towards Grindleford, Surprise and the Kinder and Upper Derwent moors.

South west is the unmistakable tuft of trees on Minninglow, whilst further away still, beyond High Tor and Masson, lies mast-crowned Alport Hill and the faint blue line marking Charnwood Forest, beyond the Trent.

Turn right at the road, for about 650yds/m, passing the junction of a lane leading back to Darley Dale and, on the left, the remains of Bond's Quarry. A short distance beyond these, an unsigned stile on the right, leads on to the moor.

Bear left, heading for the left-hand end of the trees, twisting and turning through a myriad of grooves. Fortunately the path is clear underfoot and the trees are a good guide. At the end of the moor there is a stile into Little Dog Kennel Plantation. Follow the path through the trees, across the field to the road, just opposite Moor Farm.

This place has a chequered history, having been a pub, a farm and a country club. Legend has it that the pub land- lord was a highwayman in his spare time, who met a terrible end. He had gone into the cellar to count his loot, when one of his victims returned to the pub, injured. The pub door was opened by the maid who dropped the light- ed lantern at the sight of the wounded man, igniting the building and burning the landlord to death.

Turn right along the lane until it forks. Go straight ahead on a track, which was the old Chesterfield to Darley Dale road. Follow this down through the woods, soon reaching Woodside Farm. The track becomes a tarred lane. Near the kennels turn left at a T-junction, and continue down the lane to the main road, going left to Sydnope Hall Farm. Turn right at the footpath sign pointing to Ladygrove and Farley. An arrow on a tree in mid-field marks the onward route.

Sydnope Hall lies to the left, a fine building, once

in the ownership of Sheffield City Council, but now converted into luxury flats.

The path begins to descend, and soon the ground falls away steeply to Sydnope Brook, through an area of scrub. Cross the bridge and go up the other side, to reach what was once a walled lane, but is now heavily overgrown. Turn right, soon emerging from the tangled undergrowth into a respectable walled track, running high above the valley floor.

Across the valley can be seen the old quarries at the back of Ladygrove and the houses and land where flax was dried, just by the mills.

The terraced path continues, passing an old quarry on the left and another set of Derwent aqueduct gates. When the first house is reached the track becomes a tarred lane, passing a well on the left before reaching a signpost on the right. A steep and slippery path drops to an awkward stile.

Go down to the left-hand corner of the field, then bear left to the double pylon and gates. A paved and kerbed path runs down beside the wall to Holt Farm. Turn left just beyond the farm, passing through a stile by a gate and then bearing right, heading for Enthovens' chimney. Continue to bear right, now heading to the right of the gateway to pick up a tarred path by the stream, soon reaching Oddfellows Lane.

Cross over and continue along the path alongside the garden centre, soon reaching and crossing the A6. Keep alongside the left-hand hedge past the broken sluice, skirting to the left of the DFS warehouse to Old Road. Turn right, and just before the railway bridge go right again. The path descends a flight of steps to run alongside the railway, soon reaching Station Road. (Darley Bridge car park lies 440yds/m to the left).

4 Stoney Middleton and Froggatt

The walk starts in Stoney Middleton and climbs gently to Eyam. There is a sharp ascent to the vantage point of Eyam Edge. An excellent traverse of Eyam Moor follows, with wide views. The walk then descends into Bretton and Abney Cloughs before reaching Leadmill Bridge. A pleasant stroll through woodland, alongside the Derwent, takes the walk to Grindleford and Froggatt Bridge.

Distance:
10 miles/16km
Height gain:
1,480ft/455m
Walking time:
5hours 45 minutes
Start/Finish:
Stoney Middleton (Royal Oak). GR230755. Limited parking in village. Pay and display parking in Eyam. GR216767.
Type of walk:
Packhorse trails, little-used field and moorland paths, plus easy riverside strolling. One steep, lengthy ascent.
Public transport:
Stoney Middleton has daily buses from Buxton, Sheffield and Chesterfield. Less frequent from Bakewell and Manchester. Daily trains from Manchester and Sheffield serve Hathersage and Grindleford stations.

Go along the lane at the back of the chip shop. After about 110yds/m go left, up The Fold. The lane soon degenerates into a track, which becomes a narrow, walled green lane, twisting its way

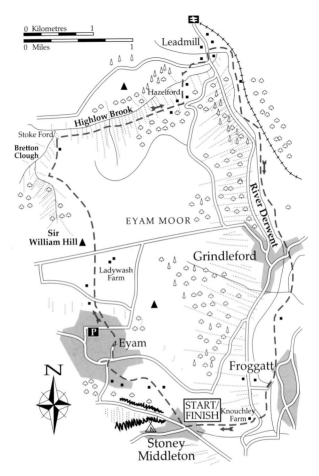

upwards and soon reaching Eyam. At the T-junction, by the barn, go right.

On the left are the Lydgate graves, one of the many

reminders of the catastrophic plague which overtook this village in the late 1660s.

At the Square, go straight across, passing the Miners Arms. Carry on up the lane, which climbs steadily until water troughs are reached. Here the lane steepens appreciably, before ending at a seat. A path continues to the left through a stile, bears away to the right, rising steadily across the slope to the top left-hand corner. Cross the road, up the steps into the wood, slanting across the slope. Skirt to the right of the youth hostel and swing right to climb even more steeply, to the top of Eyam Edge. Continue along the edge of the wood into open ground. Bear right here, soon reaching a road. Go left for about 25yds/m, then right, on to Bole Hill.

The remains of Ladywash Mine are on the right. Ladywash shaft is 800ft/255m deep, one of the deepest in Derbyshire.

The path soon reaches Sir William Hill Road. Cross, and go over a stile on to Eyam Moor. Follow the obvious path, soon reaching a cairn.

The view takes in the Losehill ridge, Kinder, the Derwent Moors, Bamford Edge, Stanage Edge and Higger Tor.

Descend steeply, heading for a gate perched on the edge of Bretton Clough. A terraced packhorse route makes for Stoke Ford, which is soon seen below. Before reaching the ford, a narrow path goes sharply to the right, contouring the steep hillside, soon joining the track coming up from Stoke Ford. Continue down the valley of Highlow Brook.

Cross a number of subsidiary streams and skirt the northern flanks of another Bole Hill, where a track is joined. Descend to the valley bottom, but do not cross the ford or footbridge. Instead go right, crossing a stream, keeping to the south side of the Highlow Brook.

Follow the obvious path, soon reaching Top Farm. Go through two sets of gates on to the farm track. In about 275yds/m, go left, descending a tarred track, leading to Hoghall. Where the track swings right, a stile straight ahead leads into fields. Follow the wall down before bearing left near the bottom to a bridge. Cross the bridge and bear right, soon climbing away from the stream to join a lane. Go right here, following the lane to the road, then descending to the Plough Inn. Go left along the B6001, crossing the Derwent at Leadmill Bridge.

This ancient crossing point was originally known as Hazelford. Earlier bridges were all victims to the turbulent nature of the Derwent winter floods, until these were tamed by the building of the dams higher up the valley in the early part of the 20th century.

Beyond the bridge, turn right along the road to Harpur Leys. At Harpur Leys, cross the bridge over the stream and bear right through the gate or stile, just before the house. Pass through open fields, cutting across a loop of the river to Coppice Wood. On emerging from the wood, the path again cuts off a bend to cross a bridge over Burbage Brook, before reaching the B6521 at Grindleford.

Go right here and just before the traffic lights, cross

a stile on the left. Bear left across the field to reach a gate in the far corner. Follow the obvious path through Froggatt Wood, a delightful mixed deciduous woodland owned by the National Trust.

After crossing a couple of substantial streams, the path emerges into open fields. An obvious path continues through a series of fields, soon passing into a narrow walled lane, leading to Froggatt village. Go down the road, turning right to cross the medieval arched bridge. Then go left, over a stile, on to the west bank of the Derwent.

At the next stile bear right, slanting up across the field to a stile in the top corner. Turn right and follow the wall to the road. Go up the lane to Knouchley Farm, keeping to the right of the main farm buildings. Just beyond the silage clamp the path goes left, heading across the field towards the lower of the two gateways, and a stile, where there is an unusual view up the hidden valley of Coombs Dale. Go over the stile and follow the wall, descending through an area of scrub and thorn. At the foot of the slope, head for the right-hand corner of the high wall surrounding Stoney Middleton Hall. A kissing gate leads into a narrow lane.

A short distance along the lane is the restored "Roman" bath house. The church on the left has an unusual octagonal nave and is dedicated to St Martin, the patron saint of cripples!

Beyond the church, head back through the village to the chip shop, main road and Royal Oak.

5 Matlock, Cromford and Masson

A deceptively easy stroll through Hall Leys Park is followed by a sharp ascent to the Heights of Abraham and Upperwood, with fine views over the Matlock Gorge. A descent to Cromford is a respite before the climb to Black Rocks, Steeple Grange and Middleton. Another descent, to the Via Gellia is inevitably followed by a stiff pull up to Slaley and Bonsall. A final climb leads up and over Masson Lees before descending, at last, to Matlock.

Distance:
8¼ miles/13km
Height gain:
2,135ft/657m
Walking time:
5½ hours
Start/Finish:
Matlock railway station. GR287602. Large car park by station.
Type of walk:
A strenuous walk with some steep ascents and descents. Generally obvious paths or packhorse routes.
Public transport:
Matlock has daily train services from Derby and daily bus services from Manchester, Stockport, Buxton, Bakewell, Chesterfield, Alfreton, Nottingham, Derby and London.

From the station, cross the bridge over the Derwent and go right, into Hall Leys Park. Follow the path through the park to Knowleston Place. Go through

a gate on the right, over Bentley Brook, passing the Knowles memorial stone. Follow the path to the right, soon passing under the railway line and continuing by the riverside to a T-junction. Turn right, crossing the Derwent to reach and cross the A6. Go left, soon bearing right, up St. John's Road and passing the chapel. Just beyond the chapel go left along the track signed to Matlock Bath, soon plunging into dense woodland.

Winter is the best time to see the towering cliffs of High Tor. The west side of the gorge is less steep, because the dip of the limestone strata runs west to east.

The path passes underneath the Matlock Bath cable cars, before reaching a lane. Go right, soon passing the entrance to the Heights of Abraham Grounds. Continue along the increasingly steep lane to Upperwood. Paths continue three ways. Follow the middle course, bearing first to the right, then left, through a signposted stile. Pass through woodland to another stile near a derelict farm. Bear right, up a sloping terrace, passing through a thicket of thorn and a stile into fields.

Go across the field to a rough lane, skirting the edge of Ball Eye Quarry. Turn left and at a junction of tracks, keep right, following the sign to Cromford. Continue beside the fence, turning right at a signpost, following a rough path down through steeply sloping woodland, across a track and into Ball Eye Wood, soon emerging into Chapel Hill Lane. Go down to the main road and pass Cromford mill pond, with its finely restored water-wheel. At the T-junction, go right, up Cromford Hill.

Pass the Bell Inn, going left at Bede House Lane. Go right by Sycamore Cottage, up a path, which climbs steeply, passing a terrace of low cottages, following signs for Black Rocks. Go left when a lane is reached, passing Holly Cottage on the right, following the rough track, until it forks.

There is a magnificent view up the Derwent valley to Matlock Bath, over towards Crich and into the depths of Dene Quarry to the west of Cromford.

Go left at the fork, following signs to Black Rocks. The path soon reaches the High Peak Trail. Turn right.

The Trail was formerly the Cromford and High Peak Railway, opened in 1830. Originally it was designed as a canal, hence the almost level stretches, punctuated by steep inclines in place of the locks.

Pass Railway Slab Rock on the right, before reaching Black Rocks picnic site. At the far end of the car park go right, to the road, skirting round the cemetery to a stile opposite GP Produce. Cross the road, passing to the left of the warehouse, following a path through rough grassland, soon bearing left to reach Dark Lane.

The hummocks and hollows in this and surrounding fields indicate lead mining activity. Between Black Rocks and this point the route has passed from gritstone, across shale and on to limestone.

Cross Dark Lane into fields, keeping straight ahead at the crossing of paths, passing to the right of the ruined building. Go straight on, to a stile by an ash tree. Cross Middleton Recreation Ground and its access track, soon dipping to a hidden stile by a capped shaft. A narrow green lane runs along the foot of a former tip, soon swinging to the right to pass between the church and the vicarage. Pass a chapel on the left and at the T-junction go right. After an initial descent, the road climbs again, passing another chapel.

There is a surprising view back, down the Ecclesbourne valley to Alport Hill and then to the distant line of Charnwood Forest.

Continue up the hill until the road levels off, turning right at the "No through road" sign. The lane soon deteriorates into a rough track. Continue past a lorry garage on the left, gently descending and keeping right at the fork. Where the lane bears left, go right, through a stile. Pass a ruin on the left, then bear right through a gateway. Follow the wall to the left, entering a walled path which soon reaches the lip of the Via Gellia.

Go left on a narrow waymarked path, soon descending steeply on slippery limestone. At the base of the slope the path loses itself in undergrowth, separated from the road by an incipient stream. Cross wherever possible to reach the road, and turn left. After 100yds/m, opposite a gateway, go right, up a slanting terrace, turning sharp left in 100yds/m. Continue up the wooded hillside to a stile into fields. Bear right at the manhole cover, up the field, through a couple of stiles, passing through a garden, to the road at Slaley. Go up more steps, before heading up to a stile in the top wall.

Skirt to the right of the house, climb the bank and follow the wall up to the gap. Head across the field to a gap in the wall by the ash tree. Now go right, diagonally across the field. Bonsall church spire is visible and forms a useful marker. Pick a way through a plethora of little fields, eventually reaching a track. Follow the track downwards, before descending a flight of steps to the road at Bonsall.

Turn right and then left at the T-junction by the cross. Pass the Kings Head, and at the cross go straight ahead, up a narrow lane, just to the right of the telephone box. Climb steeply in a deep hollow-way, until the route forks and the gradient eases. Follow the walled lane left, soon descending to a T-junction.

Turn right and recommence the climb, until a gate and stile are reached almost at the top of the hill. Go right at the signpost, straight on across a couple of fields, passing through gaps in the boundary walls. A long narrow field is followed over the brow of the hill, to a stile on to a track. Cross the track, then bear right to a stile by some limestone boulders.

This is Masson Hilltop. Left lies the Derwent valley and Stanton Moor, with Longstone Edge beyond. Ahead, spread out like a map, is Matlock.

Follow the waymarked path, down through scrub and thorn, eventually crossing the access track to Masson Lees Farm. Go over a stile into fields, following the wall/hedge down, crossing another track and continuing beside the wall/hedge, through a series of fields. Pass in front of a bunga-low and continue down through yet more stiles until the driveway to Greenhills Farm is reached. Go straight across, through another stile on to a steep field. At the bottom, the path reaches the road just where it crosses the railway. Follow the road past the Royal Bank of Scotland to the station.

6 Rowsley and Stanton Moor

A pleasant stroll through Stanton Woodhouse leads to a climb on to Stanton Moor. The eastern edge of the moor is traversed, visiting Grey's Tower and the Cork Stone. This is followed by a visit to the mysterious Nine Ladies stone circle and then a gentle descent round the northern flanks of the moor, back to Rowsley.

Distance:
5½ miles/ 9km
Height gain:
915ft/280m
Walking time:
3¼ hours
Start/Finish:
Peacock Hotel, Rowsley. GR256658. Car park just east of Peacock, off A6. GR258659.

Type of walk:
Gentle, usually on clear paths/tracks, with no difficult ascents/descents.
Public transport:
Rowsley has daily bus services from Manchester, Stockport, Buxton, Bakewell, Matlock, Derby and Nottingham.

Go down the road opposite the Peacock Hotel, passing the school. Cross the River Wye and at the road junction, go straight on, towards Stanton Woodhouse. After about 500yds/m the lane forks. Keep right here, beginning to climb steadily towards Stanton Woodhouse, passing through a copse. As the lane nears the first buildings of Stan-

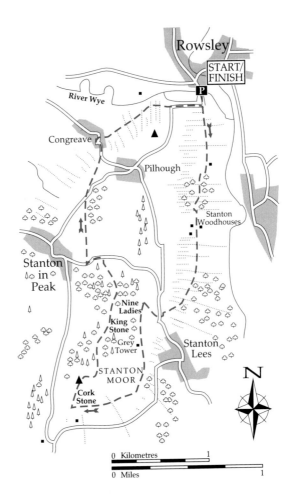

ton Woodhouse, follow a sign on the right, pointing to Stanton Lees. Go through a kissing gate and then climb alongside the wall, soon reaching another signpost, pointing through a gate on the left, to rejoin the lane. Go right, soon reaching the main part of Stanton Woodhouse. Pass through the farm complex, back into open fields.

Follow the steadily rising track across the field, rounding a shoulder of higher land to a gate. Pass through this, then follow a signposted path to the left, up the field, towards the trees, soon reaching two gates. Pass through the smaller, right-hand gate, then continue up the field. The path comes very close to the lip of a disused quarry, crosses a small field and so reaches a road.

Go right here, with the tumbled, tree-covered, rock slopes of Stanton Moor now to the left. The piles of rock are the result of long ceased gritstone quarry workings. After about 100yds/m, turn left, up a quarry track. Bear left past the ruined quarry buildings, on a path which soon climbs away from the workings, up through the trees. At the boundary of the National Trust Stanton Moor Estate go right, along a clear path, which soon crosses a stream. The path runs north through woodland, forking near the lip of another old quarry. Keep left along the more obvious, kerbed path, which heads between two sets of old workings.

The path soon leaves the workings and bears left through much older trees, soon being joined by another path from the right. The route is now heading south and at times comes quite close to the edge of the moor, which here falls away in crags, albeit man-made.

There is a good view over the valley to the eastern moors, over the tops of the trees. One particularly prominent rock has a large G carved into it; and the date 31/12/15. The moor was stripped of trees during the First World War. Perhaps this is the mark of one of those involved.

Continue along the path, ignoring a stile on the right, and, still following the wall, reach Grey's Tower.

This prominent ruined feature was erected by the local landowner, to remind the Duke of Devonshire, a Tory, of the Liberal victory and the 1832 Reform Act. Grey was the Liberal Prime Minister who brought in the Reform Bill.

Go round the back of the tower to a stile on to the moor. Bear left and follow the obvious path through the heather, passing various heather and rhododendron-covered mounds. Stanton Moor is famous for its antiquities, there being numerous hut circles, burial mounds and the famous Nine Ladies stone circle.

After about 500yds/m, keep right at the fork, heading almost south-west. Soon another path joins from the left. Climb gently, with a good view to the left, down the valley and over to Winster. On the right is one of the more prominent hut circles. Go straight on at a major crossing of tracks, over the brow of the moor to reach the Cork Stone.

From certain angles, this looks unassailable. It is shaped like the cork in a champagne bottle, overhung on all sides, but on this eastern side, steel hoops have been inserted at intervals to aid the ascent and, more particularly, the descent! Turn right by the Cork Stone, skirting the lip of a shallow quarry, bearing left where the track forks.

The western side of the moor has been quarried extensively, but the quarries are long abandoned. The path skirts several of them. On the right, scarcely higher than the path, is the trig point marking the summit of the moor.

Cut across the moor through a little patch of birch, keeping to the right at the fork and soon reaching a cross "roads". Turn right here through the birch to the Nine Ladies. Innocuous as these seem in the sunlight, in twilight, with wreaths of mist swirling round, they present a different aspect. Weird goings-on are not unknown at the Nine Ladies.

Leave the circle on the broad path leading away northwards. There is a glimpse of the television mast through the trees to the left. Keep on this broad track, passing through two gates/stiles, soon passing through fields to the road. Go left, along the lane down almost to the 30mph signs. Turn right along a signposted track, leading past the cricket ground, with a magnificent view up the Wye and Lathkill valleys.

Beyond the cricket ground the track enters woodland before emerging on the Stanton-Pilhough road. Go right, passing a well-built viewing platform on the left. Just beyond this, at a signpost, go left and descend into the adjacent field, bearing right to a gate and stile. Go straight across the next field, heading for the line of trees which mark an old boundary. Follow these to the far side of the field, where there is a discreet stile. The path follows the hedge on the right, finally deserting it to bear left to a stile, just to the left of the gate.

Here the path drops into the sunken lane. Turn left and go steeply downhill to Congreave. Go round the bends, and, at the second left-hand bend, go right, at a footpath sign, passing alongside the buildings of Dove House Farm, to a gate into open fields. Contour right, with a view across the Wye valley towards Haddon and Calton. The path rounds the nose of the hill before descending left to a stile and stream by a little wood.

Go up through the wood to a stile and into fields again. In the field, bear right, rising to meet the mound and ditch which surrounds Pic Tor, the tree clad hill on the right. An isolated post and notice marks the route. Bear left along a terrace, with the mound and ditch soon diverging to the right. The path carries on downwards to a gate and stile by the river. Here the road is rejoined and it is an easy step back to the Wye bridge and Rowsley.

The East Moors

The East Moors stretch from the gritstone ramparts of the Eastern Edges to the outskirts of Chesterfield and Sheffield. Until the enclosure of the moorland in the 18th and 19th centuries and the construction of the turnpike roads, a traverse of the East Moors was considered a major undertaking, not to be attempted without guides. The land slopes down gently from the high points of the Edges, into the main valley of the Rother, passing from the Peak District to the coalfield.

There are still swathes of heather and bilberry clad moor before the fields and woods come into their own nearer the towns. The slopes are dissected by eastward flowing streams, which have carved pleasant little valleys for themselves. Across this landscape criss-cross many old routeways. Some were upgraded to turnpikes and are now the major roads of the area; others form the backbone of the footpath and bridleway network.

Although the industry here is now farming, walkers will come across many industrial remains. Gritstone was quarried extensively. Poor quality coal was mined in shallow pits and clay was extracted for pottery and brick making. Lead was smelted on hill top "boles" before being taken eastwards to navigable water for onward transport. One of the earliest industrial chimneys still stands at Stone Edge lead smelter, visited on one of these walks. Even earlier evidence of habitation has been found, for the high moors were well populated in the Bronze Age. Settlement sites abound and the area is archaeologically very rich. The old doggerel, "When Chesterfield was gorse and broom, then Leash Fen was a market town. Now Chesterfield's the market town and Leash Fen is but gorse and broom", may yet turn out to be true.

The walks in this section explore the fine gritstone scenery of the Eastern Edges, the moorland to the east and the fields, valleys and woods adjacent to Sheffield and Chesterfield. Some of these routes are little walked, whilst others are virtual motorways. Pick your days.

7 Baslow, Chatsworth and Beeley Moors

An interesting contrast between riverbank and parkland in Chatsworth and the wilder moorland of Dobb Edge and Gardoms Edge. An easy stroll along the riverside is followed by a gentle climb up Beeley Creek on to the moor. A tramp across the moors and through the Chatsworth woods leads to Dobb Edge and Robin Hood. Further moorland and gritstone edge walking leads past the Wellington Memorial and finally down to Baslow.

Distance: 11¹/₂ miles/19km *Height gain:* 1,700ft/520m *Walking time:* 6-7hours *Start/Finish:* Baslow Nether End bus stop. GR258721. Pay and display parking near bus stop.	*Type of walk:* Easy riverbank and woodland walking, plus good moorland tracks/paths. *Public transport:* Daily buses to Baslow from Sheffield, Chesterfield, Bakewell, Buxton, Leek and the Potteries.

Baslow is a busy village in the heart of the Peak District and the gateway to Chatsworth.

Go past the little shop, following the lane leading towards Chatsworth. Go over the bridge and turn right, alongside the Bar Brook. At the end of the lane go along the signposted path to Chatsworth.

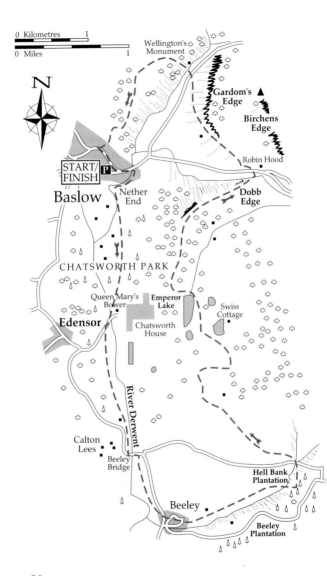

0 Kilometres 1
0 Miles 1

N

Wellington's
Monument

Gardom's
Edge

Birchens
Edge

Robin Hood

START/
FINISH P

Baslow

Nether
End

Dobb
Edge

CHATSWORTH PARK

Queen Mary's
Bower

Edensor

Emperor
Lake

Swiss
Cottage

Chatsworth
House

River Derwent

Calton
Lees

Beeley Bridge

Beeley

Hell Bank
Plantation

Beeley
Plantation

This narrow track soon reaches a kissing gate of monumental proportions leading into Chatsworth Park. An almost level path leads through the park with glimpses of the house through the trees.

On the hillside is the Hunting Tower. This is a remnant of the Elizabethan Chatsworth that was demolished to make way for the 18th-century palace that is Chatsworth House.

Pass White Lodge on the right and skirt the cricket pitch. Queen Mary's Bower comes into view, to the right of the House.

The Bower is also an Elizabethan survival. In it the unfortunate Mary, Queen of Scots was allowed to enjoy the fresh air and views of the Park whilst still being closely guarded. The Bower is surrounded by a moat and has only one access. To the right is the River Derwent, which cuts through the centre of the Park and forms one of the main features of this attractive landscape.

Go past the Bower to the road, turning right to cross the lovely 18th-century bridge. Once over the bridge turn left, following the broad path along the river bank, soon passing two large weirs and a ruined water-mill. The mill lost its roof when a tree fell on it in a severe gale in the 1960s. Keep a sharp lookout for deer, which are often seen roaming on the far (private) bank.

Continue alongside the river to a kissing gate close to the lodge and Beeley Bridge. Go over the bridge, then through a kissing gate to the right. An obvious path bears away from the river.

The green dome structures on the left are access ways to valves on the Derwent Aqueduct which carries water from the Derwent Dams down to Derby, Nottingham and Leicester. The view ahead encompasses Beeley Moor to the left and Stanton Moor with Grey's Tower to the right.

Bear left to another kissing gate opposite Beeley Church. Cross the road and go up the lane beside the church into the village. At the T-junction turn right and then left at the triangle. Pass the old school and keep left at the fork in the road. Continue along the narrow lane, passing a log cabin on the right. Keep left where the track forks, passing Moor Farm to the right.

The track begins to climb steadily. Pass through another gate and continue beside the wood. Ignore the first two gates into the wood and go straight on. Pass through a third gate, then bear right at a gate/stile and enter the wood.

The path descends to cross a stream, then climbs through the birch wood, with Beeley Brook churning away below. The path steepens, passing some larger boulders before reaching a broader track. Turn left along a broad ride through the trees, with a glimpse of the moor ahead, soon reaching a lane. Go over the stile on to the open moor, signposted to Robin Hood.

From the moor top there is a magnificent view across to the west and to the north. The path soon leads down to a gate at the boundary of Chatsworth Park. Follow the obvious track which is signposted at critical points to Robin Hood, through Stand Woods, and eventually passing Swiss Lake on the right.

After skirting the Emperor Lake on the left, the water supply to the famous Emperor fountain, the path just misses the Elizabethan Hunting Tower. It is too good to leave out, so visit the tower then return to the path, still following signs to Robin Hood. Where the lane swings right to Parkgate, go straight on, soon emerging from the woodland.

There is a fine view over to Birchens Edge, where the Three Ships and Nelson's Monument can be clearly seen. Soon the view extends over to Baslow Edge, Wellington Monument and the Eagle Stone.

Stroll along Dobb Edge. There is one "exciting" bit where there are fixed ropes, unusual, if not unique, in the Peak District. The path soon descends to cross Heathylea Brook before reaching the A619, near the Robin Hood pub. Cross the road and follow the signposted path on to the moor, rising gently through rock outcrops on the edge of Heathylea Plantation, to a fine vantage point near a narrow gateway.

Baslow can be seen below and the view extends to High Rake. The eye is drawn to the stand of trees, planted in Coronation year, which make the letters E.R.

The path descends to the A621 near Cupola Cottage, a former lead smelt. Cross the road, go over the stile opposite, rapidly descending to cross the bridge over Bar Brook. Climb past a bungalow, into rough ground below Wellington's Monument, an area known as Jack Flat. Still rising, the path swings to the left, soon reaching the main edge path. Turn right to visit the monument and the Eagle Stone.

Legend has it that the Eagle Stone was the local test for manhood. A youth could only marry a Baslow girl if he had first climbed the stone.

Retrace your steps from the stone or monument and descend the obvious route towards Baslow. The track soon becomes a metalled road and enters the village. At the triangle of roads with the tree and seat in the middle, go left, along Eaton Hill, to Nether End.

8 Fox House and the Eastern Edges

This must be one of the easiest high-level walks. The bus ride from Baslow to Fox House does most of the climbing. The walk is then little more than a delightful stroll along the spectacular Eastern Edges, with grand views over the Derwent valley and the central hills of the Peak District, before descending to Baslow.

Distance:
6¼ miles/10km
Height gain:
420ft/130m
Walking time:
3½ hours.
Start:
Fox House Inn. Pay parking at Longshaw.
Finish:
Baslow Nether End. GR258721. Pay and display by bus stop.
Maps:
Outdoor Leisure Nos. 1 Dark Peak, and 24

White Peak.
Type of walk:
Easy walk on well-defined paths in spectacular surroundings. No significant climbing, but optional scrambling.
Public transport:
Fox House has daily bus services from Sheffield, Bakewell, Baslow, Castleton and the Hope valley villages. For Baslow services see walk 7.

This walk begins in Sheffield. From the bus stop, go past the pub, cross the road, go through a small gate marked with a National Trust sign and enter Derbyshire, and Longshaw Estate. Stroll down to the lodge gates and turn left, soon reaching the NT information centre. There is a fine view to the right from here, across to Millstone Edge, Mother Cap and the upper section of Padley Brook. Pass to the right of the centre and the hunting lodge, along a signposted path, which soon forks. Keep left, passing through a small gate on to a broad track. Bowl along the track admiring the view to the right.

Higger Tor and Carlwark are prominent features, whilst to the left, on the skyline, is the slender shape of Longshaw Pole, a timber guide post dating back to packhorse times. This area was formerly part of the Duke of Rutland's estates. The track was the main carriage drive to the hunting lodge.

Pass between the large stone gateposts and soon enter an area of thin mixed woodland. At the crossing of tracks go straight ahead along the carriage drive, soon passing through a gate leading into more open country.

The view to the right has now changed, for the track has swung south. Sir William Hill, with the old turnpike route very clearly defined, can be seen. Ahead looms the scarp of White Edge.

Still bearing left, the drive soon reaches the road. Go right, and after 100yds/m go right again, into a rough field. Bear left to a stile by the National Trust sign. From here the view is of the Hope and Upper Derwent valleys, with Win Hill and Bamford Edge clearly visible.

Follow the clear path on top of the ridge, going left at the wall corner, into a woodland of birch,

START

Fox House Inn

Longshaw Lodge

Nether Padley

River Derwent

Froggatt Edge

White Edge

Cubar Edge

Froggatt

Curber

Baslow Edge

Eagle Stone

Cliff College

Wellington's Monument

Baslow

FINISH

Nether End

0 Kilometres 1

0 Miles 1

N

sycamore and mountain ash, which masks all views. The path passes to the right of the National Trust car park, before swinging to the left and descending steeply to cross a stream. Go up steps on the far bank to reach the road again. Go right, crossing to the kissing gate leading onto Froggatt Edge.

The walk along the Eastern Edges is one of the classics of the Peak District. It is so easy and yet so magnificent. It starts through woodland with few clues as to the view. There are occasional clusters of rocks, some big enough to scramble on. Then, at a gate, the path leaves the trees, coming on to open moor with the land falling away steeply to the right.

The view is very extensive, across and down the Derwent valley. So delightful is this vista that it is easy to miss the stone circle on the left, a reminder that man has used these moors for millennia. Soon the limestone quarries near Stoney Middleton come into view and beyond them High Rake. Froggatt village lies below, whilst southwards the view stretches to Hassop Common and Ball Cross near Bakewell.

The track soon passes through a cluster of rocks and the highest point on the walk comes into view ahead. The edge falls away precipitously to the right, though there are routes down, even for walkers. Chatsworth House and Calton Lees now come into view as the path skirts a nick in the edge, the route of an old packhorse track. The rock scenery is dramatic.

Where the main track begins to bear away from the edge, a narrow path continues ahead. Follow this, but keep a sharp look out as some of the gaps between the rocks are much deeper than might be imagined. In one case there is a four foot wide cleft, twenty to thirty feet deep. Keep young children firmly under control! All too soon this exciting path rejoins the main route at the high point.

There is a good view back to the moors round Longshaw. Ahead lies Curbar Edge, with Curbar village below to the right. In the distance the Eagle Stone and Wellington Monument can be seen on Baslow Edge, with the Nelson Monument further away on Birchens Edge.

The broad track leads unerringly to Curbar Gap, but it is worth deviating closer to the edge for the views down. At the Gap, cross the road and go up the track opposite, on to Baslow Edge, with a view straight up Middleton Dale to Eyam and Tideslow. The main path keeps well away from the edge, but a much narrower path bears right and keeps to the lip of the crags.

Despite missing out the Eagle Stone, this route is greatly to be preferred. It rejoins the main route just south of the Eagle Stone, having skirted the edge of a small disused quarry. At the main track go right and follow this route down into Baslow, being sure to turn left at the triangular junction with the tree in the middle. Eaton Hill leads down to Nether End and the finish of the walk.

9 Holmesfield and Barlow

A stroll through fields from Holmesfield, leads down to the hamlet of Millthorpe. A gradual ascent then leads via Barlow Woodseats, to Moorhall. Grange Lumb and Barlow Grange are visited and little-used paths round Oxton Rakes explored. The ascent of Bolehill is followed by a descent to Barlow with grand views. The walk concludes by a gradual climb back to Holmesfield along a fine green lane.

Distance:	GR317765.
7½ miles/12km	**Type of walk:**
Height gain:	Field and woodland
1,480ft/455m	paths, plus old
Walking time:	packhorse routes, some
4-5 hours	very little used. No
Start/Finish:	difficult ascents.
Holmesfield, Travellers	**Public transport:**
Rest. GR322777.	Holmesfield has daily
Limited roadside	buses from Sheffield
parking in village.	and a Monday to
Alternative roadside	Saturday service from
parking at Millthorpe,	Chesterfield.

Walk up the B6054 towards the church. Go left down the signposted footpath between the George and Dragon and other buildings, soon reaching open fields. There is a fine view up the Cordwell Valley to the eastern moors of the Peak. Keep straight on, descending gently towards Millthorpe. In the second field the path follows the left-hand

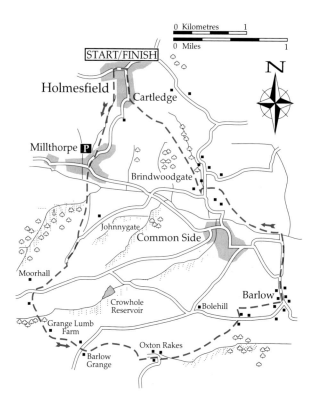

boundary, a hedge, reinforced by a very deep ditch. Carry on down two fields alongside the stream, to a bridge and stile. Continue to follow the stream down, eventually reaching a gate into a sunken track, leading on to the road to Millthorpe. At Millthorpe, go down the lane on the right of the cafe, crossing Millthorpe Brook. Continue up the narrowing lane and, where the track turns right to

Mill Farm, go right, over a stile. Keep alongside the left-hand hedge, beside the narrow hollow-way.

The hollow-way is paralleled by a footpath for most of its length. The justification was the heavy use of the bridleway and its usual muddy state. Alternative parallel footpaths developed on higher, drier ground alongside. In Cordwell valley the bridleways see heavy horse use and the alternative footpaths serve their original purpose.

At the next stile bear right to a bridge over Dingle Dike, then keep to the left, by the hedge, climbing all the while. A gateway and stile by an oak leads to another field. Head towards the redundant stile in mid-field, then down to the stream, where cattle cross. Go further upstream, passing between two trees, crossing the stream at a less muddy point. Go up past a holly tree, then fork right to join a rough lane, almost opposite Barlow Woodseats. Turn right, passing through Hollin Wood, then up a hollow-way, eventually reaching Moorhall.

Cross the road and follow the footpath sign opposite, climbing through a narrow field, alongside Bank Farm, through a white gate near a pylon. Carry straight on, negotiating a stile, and bear left to Grange Wood. In the wood the path crosses Grange Lumb Brook, and soon regains open fields. Grange Lumb Farm lies to the left. The place name "lumb" means "a steep-sided wooded valley"; very appropriate in this case.

Go straight ahead to a stile by the sycamore tree, crossing the farm access. Head for a gap and stile in the holly hedge, then continue upwards, bearing right, until a stile and gate are reached.

There is a good view back towards the Peak District hills and an equally good view to the east over Chesterfield and Sheffield.

Follow the obvious track about 500yds/m to the road, opposite the lane to Barlow Grange. Go left at a signpost near the Grange and follow the fence and wall down, through a couple of stiles. Go straight on across the middle of the next field, with a pylon as a useful marker, to a stile in the corner. Cross a narrow lane and go through the gate, following the hedge to a stile by an ash tree. A narrow, fenced path skirts a gas tank to reach a drive. There is a signposted stile to the right of the ornamental gates.

A sketchy path bears right to a hidden stile in the hedge. Bear left, passing the ornamental pond, to a culvert in the bottom corner. The indistinct path climbs to a stile to the right of a pylon, before following the hedge to a green lane. Go left here, and left again at the road to arrive at Oxton Rakes.

Go through the hamlet to the junction. Turn left down the green lane, descending to cross a small stream. Go over a well-hidden stile in the wall on the right, then bear left, heading uphill towards the small barn. Newgate Farm soon comes into view and the path heads for it. Where a track swings into the farm, keep straight on, skirting to the left of the buildings, to a stile by a large sycamore. The path runs along the back of the farm to the road.

Walk along the road for a short distance, before turning left at a signpost, indicating a narrow path with steps, which passes between buildings into fields. Bear left to a gateway, following the wall up to the brow of the hill, to a stile on the right. Go right and commence the descent to Barlow.

Go down the middle of the field heading for the gateway, with the church tower of St. Lawrence, Barlow, soon in view and forming a useful marker. The path runs virtually straight, until the church-yard wall is reached. Here the path bears right, passing a side gate to enter the village. Turn left along the road.

Where the main road swings left, carry straight on along a narrow lane, passing Elm Tree Farm. Follow the lane down to Lee Bridge, crossing Barlow Brook. Ignore the first gateway on the left but take the next path on the left into the wood. When the wood is left behind, the path squirms through scrub, before re-entering woodland. Continue through the wood to a green lane, and then a road, there turning right.

In less than 100yds/m, go left at a signpost into a rough field. Descend through scrub, down a flight of steps, into the back garden of a house, where further steps lead down to the drive. Follow the drive round to the right of the house, to join a lane and go right. The lane rapidly degenerates to a track and the walker is faced with a bridlegate and stile. The bridleway rises steadily between high hedges and fences, sometimes even on a low embankment. After 3/4 mile/(1.2 km), where a farm track joins, the bridleway becomes a lane but continues to climb, before reaching Cartledge Hall Farm. Follow Cartledge Lane, passing the superb Jacobean Cartledge Hall on the right. Millthorpe Lane joins from the left and from here it is but 400yds/m level going into the centre of Holmesfield.

10 Kelstedge and Spitewinter

From Kelstedge the walk passes through a picturesque section of the Upper Amber valley. Gentle climbing leads to a high point at Alicehead, Stone Edge Smelter, the House-under-the-Rock and Stone Edge. Little-used field paths lead back to Ashover, and Kelstedge.

Distance:
6¾ miles/11km.
Height gain:
815ft/250m
Walking time:
4 hours
Start/Finish:
Kelstedge bus stop.
GR339637. Limited roadside parking in village. Alternative parking at Stone Edge, GR340672.

Type of walk:
Easy woodland and field paths, some very little used. No steep ascents/descents.
Public transport:
Daily bus services to Kelstedge from Matlock and Chesterfield. Monday to Saturday service from Clay Cross.

Go down Vernon Lane opposite the Kelstedge Inn. Where it turns left to Amber House, continue ahead, along a waymarked, narrow track, soon entering a wood. Cross the clapper bridge over the infant Amber, and bear right, up a rough field, keeping the stream to the right and the fence to the left. In about 330yds/m the path reaches a lane. Turn left to the junction signposted to Stone Edge. Turn right here and soon cross the Amber again.

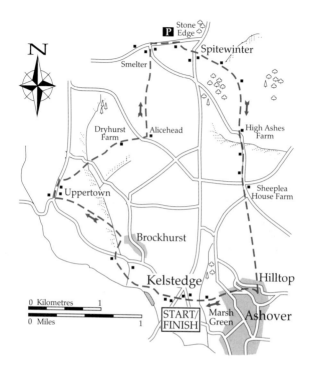

Less than 100yds/m beyond the bridge, turn left at a gateway, which has no footpath sign and looks like a private drive. Skirt to the right of the buildings, past the standing stone and on to the mill dam through a kissing gate.

Go along the top of the dam, then alongside the mill leat, through a rough field and into a wood. In the wood the path winds through the trees, before reaching the stream. There is no bridge, but the stream is narrow. On the other bank bear right, following the stream, then climbing to the left to reach open fields. Proceed alongside a wood before passing through a gateway on the right. Turn left, following the fence/hedge to a stile in the field corner. Carry straight on, through a series of fields, to Uppertown. Turn right here, along the road, passing the Social Centre. Just after the last house, go right at an unsigned stile. Head across the field to the far right-hand corner, then make for the left of the blockwork hut and right of the bungalow, to reach a lane.

Cross on to a rough track and immediately seek for a hidden stile on the right. Head up the fields, keeping to the left of the Dryhurst Farm, soon joining the access track, bearing right at this point. Pass through the farm complex, heading for Alicehead and the road. Go right at the road. Take the first track left, skirting round Alicehead Farm to reach fields again. Bear left to a stile in the left-hand wall, heading towards the television mast.

This is the highest point on the walk and the view is extensive. Sir William Hill, near Grindleford, can easily be distinguished, and the moorlands near Fox House. The tower blocks on the outskirts of Sheffield seem very close, whilst to the east are the Trent valley power stations. Closer at hand is the chimney of the Stone Edge lead smelter.

Make a bee line for the chimney and once on the open moor, the path is paved. A final stile leads into the land surrounding the smelter, where heather and scrub has run riot. Continue to head for the chimney, turning right at the wall, to reach a lane. Turn left, go down to the main road and turn right. Pass the Toads Mouth Rock on the left.

Just beyond the Red Lion is the House-under-the-Rock. The rock outcrop behind the house is Stone Edge, which is partly natural and partly quarried.

Just beyond the pub car park entrance, go right, along a driveway, to a gate. Pass to the right of the house and the Nissen hut, before following a wall to the A632. Go straight on down the side of a house, through a very rough field to a stile. Bear right, through thorn and gorse, to a stile. Head across the field to a stile by the oak and holly trees. A muddy path leads past the farm to a track.

Go right for a short distance then left by another oak, alongside the wall to a stile on the left. Turn right, alongside the wall/fence to another stile, then bear right, towards Hazelhurst Farm. Go through the gate into the farm yard, bearing right on to a track. Follow the track until it swings right, then go straight ahead, through a stile. Follow the hedge to another stile, which simply swaps the path from one side of the hedge to the other.

At High Ashes Farm, pass the farmhouse and go through an ornamental gateway to reach the road. Go left, passing Spancarr Farm. At Sheeplea House crossroads, about 100yds/m beyond Spancarr, go straight across for about another 220yds/m, until the lane forks. In the cruck of the fork is a stile. Head straight across two fields, almost due south, then bear left across a third field, heading to the left of the trees on the skyline. Just before reaching the corner, there is a stile on the left. Follow the wall to the right and then go left to reach the way-marked exit stile.

Straight on, following a wall on the left. Go through a gateway on the left, heading diagonally right, to a stile lying to the left of a gateway in the right-hand corner. Continue to a stile by a large bush, then follow the wall to a lane. Turn right, but in less than 100yds/m go left by a big boulder, soon reaching another lane. Go straight ahead, down a tarred path, which soon becomes a lane. Go right at the T-junction, passing Marshall Cottage. Go left at the fork, down Chapel Hill. At the T-junction go right, then immediately left into fields.

Go down by the wall, swopping sides part way, soon reaching a lane. Go right here, but go left at Marsh Green House, following the signposted footpath. Cross Marsh Brook, before rising sharply to join the Ashover to Kelstedge road. Go right here, to reach Kelstedge.

11 Matlock to Ashover and back

Start easily through Hall Leys Park and Matlock Green before striking uphill through Lumsdale, over "The Pine Ridge" to Lant Lodge Farm, Old Engine Farm and Cocking Tor. A steep descent to Ravenhouse Farm is followed by Ashover Hay and a steady pull to Highoredish and Mathersgrave. Wheatcroft, Lea, Dethick and Riber are all visited, then a sharp descent leads to Old Matlock and Matlock Station.

Distance:
13¼ miles/21km
Height gain:
2,110ft/650m
Walking time:
7 hours
Start/Finish:
Matlock railway station. GR287602. Large car park by station.
Maps:
Outdoor Leisure

No.24 White Peak. Pathfinder No.761 Chesterfield and No.794 Crich and Bullbridge.
Type of walk:
A long walk with some steep ascents/descents. Mainly easy to follow paths and tracks.
Public transport:
For services to Matlock see walk 5.

Follow the same route from the railway station as walk 5, but at Knowleston Place, carry straight on to Matlock Green. Continue along the Tansley road, turning left at Butts Drive. A tarred path

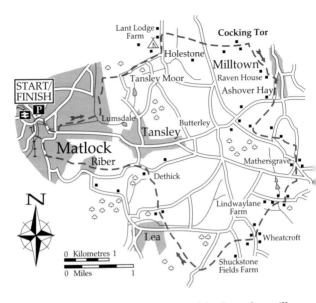

skirts the edge of the playing fields. Pass the mills on the right before descending to the Lumsdale road. Go left here, climbing through another set of mill buildings, before reaching ruined mills on the left, by a bridge. This complex of old mills is in the care of the Arkwright Society, who allow access to most of the site.

Go through a gate on the right, ascending the flight of steps above the stream, through the mill complex, soon reaching a track by the dam and passing the row of cottages. The gradient eases and another overgrown dam is passed.

There is a surprisingly deep valley to the left, but it has no stream. At some time in the distant past the stream was diverted on to its present course, thereby giving a much bigger head of water for the mills.

Bear right near Beech House, soon reaching some stepping stones. Go up the rough path on the far bank until the path forks by the wall corner. Straight on here, still climbing, into the pine trees. The path wriggles its way through the tree clad old tips, soon emerging into a rough field. Keep to the right of this field to a lane. After ³/₄ mile/1km, turn left at a T-junction, along Lant Lane. In 350yds/m go right at a signpost, following the path/track across two fields into a shallow valley. Bear right, making for the silage tower of Old Engine Farm and passing Windmill Pond, before reaching the road. Go right, passing the farm entrance.

Old Engine Farm takes its name from the pumping engine that was once sited here to raise water from Gregory Mine.

Just past the farm entrance go left at the footpath sign, heading just to the right of the copse of trees. Skirt to the right of the copse, then bear right to a stile at the head of Cocking Tor. A steep and sometimes very slippery descent follows, before reaching the overgrown spoil heaps of Gregory Mine. Pick a way through the spoil tips, soon passing the cottages and the old washery. Continue for 350yds/m, then turn right at a junction. Cross the rough, muddy patch, to a stile left of two fir trees.

Follow the wall to a narrow lane. Opposite is a stile back into fields. Pass the gatepost with the holes and cross the slippery bridge, through a couple of fields before Raven House Farm comes into view. Head straight across the field towards the farm, then skirting to the right of the buildings to a lane. Go left, passing the farm, continuing along the lane, soon passing Greenfield Farm on the right. Just beyond the drive, go right at an unsigned gate. Pick a way through three fields, with a couple of awkward stiles, before reaching a road.

Bear right, following the road to a T-junction with the B6014. Go through a gate opposite, into a green lane running down to a ford. An indistinct path follows the left-hand side of the stream to a double stile in the hedge. Go across the field, through the stile in the wall and go left, plodding up the field to the top left corner, just before the farm. Go left here, then immediately right, passing the barn and going through the farmyard to the access road. Follow it to the left, skirting Highoredish. The track levels out and is joined by a lane coming up from Rough Close Farm. Carry on to Highoredish Farm, then follow the sign to Trinity Chapel.

Follow the left-hand fence to a waymarked stile, then descend by the side of the wood. Two further stiles bring the path to Whitecarr Lane. Turn right, following the road to Mathersgrave.

This is a pleasant little spot, with a trough and an old guide stoop dated 1730. The nearby datestone with the initials SM refer to the suicide, Samuel Mather, from whom the hamlet gets its name.

Bear left at the next junction, along the Wessington

road. In 100yds/m, bear right on to a green lane which leads to The Plough. Cross the A615 and go over the stile, following the left-hand wall to a stile/gate. Head left across the next field, keeping left of the thorn bush and right of the holly, to locate a stile. Follow the left-hand hedge to a stile, then bear diagonally right, soon passing through the gate into the farm yard, then left on to a track. Almost at once go right, over a stile, following the wall down to a gate on to a track round the reservoir. Go left, but just beyond the dam bear right, over the grass to reach Lindway Lane. Go right, cross the bridge and just beyond the buildings, go left, over a stile, back into fields. Bear right to reach a bridge and stile in the far right-hand corner. Bear right again, climbing to the gateway in the top left-hand corner. Still on the same course, head diagonally across the next field to a track in the top left-hand corner.

At Beech Farm a grandiose stile leads into the hamlet of Wheatcroft. Go left, but where the road bears left, go straight on, along the track, passing Alma Cottage and bearing right. A stile on the left leads into fields. Turn right and climb up through the trees towards Mount Pleasant Farm. At the top of this hill go through a stile in the corner. Follow the wall to the right, before going through a stile on the right, then turning left to the road.

Go through the stile opposite, following the left-hand wall, continuing through a series of stiles and entering a large field. Go straight on, heading towards the barn. In the next field, bear right, towards Alport Hill, thus locating a stile in the field corner. Keep slightly right of the wall to reach a stile, bearing right across the next field, heading to the left of the gap in the wall, where there is another stile. Go diagonally right and down the field towards the solitary tree. The stile on to the road is to the right of the gate.

Turn left briefly, then go right, following the sign to Dethick. Continue through a series of fields, with Lea now in view ahead, before bearing left to a well hidden stile by a large oak and entering a deep hollow-way. Turn right, but just past the engraved stone, climb left to leave the hollow-way.

Bear right, heading towards Dethick church, cutting across the fields, before reaching a track which parallels the main road through Lea. Turn right by the garage to the main road. Go left and cross to a stile signposted to Tansley. Cross the Lea Brook, before climbing through the wood into open fields. Head directly for the church, across two fields.

Dethick church and the nearby farm are associated with the Babbington family and the ill-fated plot to assassinate Queen Elizabeth I and put Mary Stuart on the throne.

Pass to the right of the church, then left, down the farm access to the road. Go over the stile opposite. Keeping the wall on the left, pass through a series of fields, until the path curves right to a white gate and a rough lane. Turn right to reach the road. Turn left, following the lane for 350yds/m, bearing left at the junction for another 300yds/m. At a slight left-hand bend go over an unsigned stile on the right and turn left, following the wall through a series of fields, heading straight for Riber. Eventually the path joins a broad green lane, following this past the farm. After 150yds/m, leave the lane by a stile on the left and follow the path through fields to the village.

Go right at the road, bearing left at the T-junction near the Manor. Pass the mock medieval gate turret, and just before the gateway go right, with the castle wall on the left. At the next stile, there is a tremendous view across Matlock and right up the Derwent valley. Proceed down the very steep, paved path, soon bearing left to ease the gradient and eventually passing along a fenced way between two schools to reach Starkholmes Road.

Turn right and go down the road almost to the Duke William. At 132 Church Street, go left, down a lane, soon passing under the railway line to reach the Derwent. Cross the bridge and turn right to the railway station.

12 Wadshelf and Linacre

A gentle walk through attractive and little-frequented countryside. The paths south of Old Brampton, through Loads to Wadshelf, are lovely and quiet. Linacre Reservoirs and Linacre Woods are delightful. Easy field paths lead back to Old Brampton.

Distance:
7 miles/11 km
Height gain:
1,475 ft/455m
Walking time:
4 hours 15 minutes
Start/Finish:
Old Brampton Church. GR336719. Limited roadside parking in village. Alternative parking at

Linacre Woods picnic site, GR336727.
Type of walk:
Easy walking on field paths and green lanes, with few route-finding difficulties.
Public transport:
Old Brampton has daily bus services from Chesterfield, Baslow and Bakewell.

From the church go down the Chesterfield road for 200yds/m before turning right through an unsigned gateway. Follow the track which soon descends into the valley bottom. Cross the stream and ascend to the T-junction near Broomhall Farm. Here go left, then through a gate on the right, passing the barn and following the fence. Near the end of the field, bear slightly right to a stile. Follow the hedge, passing through a signposted stile and skirting to the left of the farm. At the end of the field there is a stile

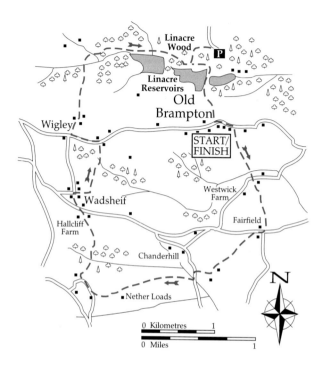

on the right and the path then follows the hedge on the left, soon reaching the A619.

Turn right for about 150yds/m until The Yews is reached. Cross the road and go down the track opposite, which skirts to the right of Burley House, soon becoming a narrow, hedged lane. In a little over 100yds/m, the track swings to the left and a footpath goes off to the right. Follow this path, through the bushes into the field and bear left to the far side of the field where there is a stile and ditch. The footpath continues across the next field, keeping on the same alignment. Go through the stile at the far right-hand corner of the field and head towards the waymarked pylon and solitary tree, cresting a rise to reveal a gateway.

Follow the left-hand hedge, going right at the next gate, crossing the field to pass through a gap in the hedge in the far corner. Go immediately right, through a stile. Bear left across the field to reach a stile by two trees, thus reaching the access to Woodhead Farm and then a lane. Go left and descend the deep hollow-way. Where the lane bears left, follow the footpath sign on the right, pointing to Chanderhill. Descend to the stream, before turning left at a stile. Pass through a large holly bush (!), before going sharp right to a bridge.

Follow the path up beside the fence and wood on the right. A steady plod uphill soon reaches the end of the wood. Follow the fence and hedge on the left, soon passing into the fringe of Birkinshaw Wood.

The path emerges from the wood to follow the hedge on the left. After about 100yds/m, look out for another stile on the left, leading into Back Wood. Here the path immediately forks. Bear right and follow a sketchy path which winds through the trees, crossing a number of ditches. At the edge of the wood, bear right. Go up the field, through patches of gorse and thorn to the top corner, then following the hedge to the right. Continue through a number of fields, until Besom Farm is reached. Skirt round to the right of the farm to reach the road.

Head for Loads House Farm, bearing right along the access track and then right again where the track forks. A stile on the right leads into fields. Skirt to the right of the farm buildings, then keep about 50yds/m from the left-hand edge of the field, heading down the slope and soon entering Hagg Wood.

Cross the bridge and climb steeply, but where an obvious track goes off to the right, continue straight ahead up a half-hidden path to the top of the wood and the exit stile. Follow the fence on the right to the stile by the tree. Follow the track to the left, passing through a series of stiles, to Hallcliff Farm where the track becomes a lane. A stile on the right takes the path round the farm buildings to a short flight of steps into another lane. Go straight across into fields again. Cross three fields to the A619. Cross the road and go left briefly before going right, through an unmarked stile. Follow the wall down the field to the bottom, then up a narrow, walled way, soon reaching Wadshelf, by the chapel.

Go right and follow the lane down past Ivy Cottage Farm. About 200yds/m from the junction, go left through an unsigned stile, following the wall and crossing it in about 100yds/m. Continue alongside the wall, bearing right at the next stile and crossing the field to the middle of the far wall. Go towards the obvious remains of a spoil heap. Cross the track into the former workings. Go left, following the base of the tip, and climb one of the numerous cattle paths to the top to locate a vehicle track. Follow this to the road, almost opposite the Royal Oak. Go left to the cross roads by Wigley school and then turn right, soon passing Wigley Farm.

There is an unusual view to the left from here, towards Longshaw and the moors near Fox House.

On reaching Wigley Hall Farm, follow the sign pointing to Linacre Reservoirs. Descend the bridleway which soon levels out and fords a stream. Go straight ahead on a narrow path, crossing the Birley Brook and entering open fields. Go right, closely following the stream, crossing a subsidiary trickle. Keep right where the path forks, following the base of the bank until the boundary wall of the water company property is reached. A short climb to the left reveals a ladder stile.

Go into the wood, following the delightful path which soon reaches a much larger track forming the reservoir perimeter walk. Keep on the north side of the lake, a lovely walk. Soon the wall of the top dam can be seen ahead and the path swings left to bridge a small inlet. The path then forks. Here there are different routes for bus and car users.

If you are a bus user, continue ahead along the lower path until the wall of the second dam is reached and then turn right.

The next paragraph is for car users only:

Turn left here and then right along the higher path, which leads away from the lakes, soon coming close to the boundary wall of the wood. A left turn at a flight of steps leads unerringly back to the car park. Starting from Linacre Woods car park, follow the tarred path through the wood then down the flight of steps with occasional glimpses of the reservoir below. Soon the path emerges onto the reservoir perimeter track, close to the dam wall. Go left here and then right at the dam.

All users: Cross the dam and go left, descending briefly, then rising to a junction. Go right, up steps to a stile. Beyond a clump of gorse Old Brampton church comes into view. Follow the obvious path to a rough lane which soon reaches Old Brampton. Turn left to the church or the George and Dragon.

The Dove, Lower Hamps and Manifold Valleys

The Dove and Manifold rise within a few yards of one another, near Flash Bar, while the Hamps starts further south near Morridge. At its source in the gritstones and shales, the Dove valley is narrow and steep sided. Paths criss-cross the stream but this area is little walked. It is a harsh landscape, with no villages and only scattered farms, but the number of ruins, paths and obvious packhorse routes, tell of a more frequented past.

The transition from moorland stream to dale river is sudden, for at Hollinsclough the Dove enters the limestone. Here are the spectacular reef hills of Hollin, Parkhouse and Chrome, whose serrated tops would do credit to much higher mountains. These hills are a geologist's paradise, former coral reefs in a tropical sea. From here on there is a good path along the valley bottom, becoming busier the further south one goes.

Beyond Crowdecote the Dove valley widens out, but still with the limestone on the east. By the time Hartington is reached the valley is so broad that it almost joins with that of the Manifold, for here the two are running through softer shales.

From Hartington the Dove again runs through grand limestone scenery, the popular Wolfscote and Berresford Dales, before entering Dovedale proper. The best-known features of this dale are contained in this lower section, Ilam Rock, the Twelve Apostles, etc. The path is broad and busy. Nowhere more so than at the famous stepping stones near Thorpe Cloud, just before the confluence with the Manifold.

The Hamps and Manifold do not enter the limestone until Waterhouses and Hulme End respectively. Walks in their upper and middle reaches come into the Staffordshire Moorlands section of this book. At Hulme End and Waterhouses the scenery changes from rolling gritstone and shale valleys to dramatic limestone. These two places were the termini of the former Leek and Manifold Light Railway, closed in the 1930s. The line ran along the valleys of the Hamps and Manifold, necessitating numerous bridges. The trackbed is now a road so these sections are very accessible. This is limestone scenery at its best, with towering cliffs and caves. Both rivers vanish, sinking into holes in their beds except during winter.

Beyond the junction with the Hamps, the Manifold valley ceases to be accessible, with only occasional paths crossing it until Ilam is reached. At this point the river re-emerges, flowing past this lovely limestone village to join the Dove. After the Dove and Manifold join, the scenery changes completely, coming out of the limestone into softer rocks. The transition from Peak District to Midlands is sudden and complete.

13 Ashbourne and Dovedale

A stroll along the Tissington Trail and Spend Lane leads to a descent into Dovedale. A strenuous ascent near Ilam Rock is followed by a fine ramble over Bunster to Ilam and along the riverbank to Ashbourne.

Distance:
13½ miles/23km (12 miles/20km for car users)
Height gain:
2,030ft/625m (1,960 ft/555m for car users)
Walking time:
7-8 hours (7 hours for car users)
Start/Finish:
Ashbourne Bus Station. GR179464. Pay and display parking in town, or Mappleton Lane car park GR176469.

Maps:
Outdoor Leisure No.24 White Peak and Pathfinder 810 Ashbourne and Churnet valley.
Type of walk: A long walk, mainly on field and riverside paths, but with some steep climbing.
Public transport: Daily buses to Ashbourne from Derby, Belper, Leek, London and Manchester.

From the bus station go through the Market Square, following the signs to Mappleton Lane car park on the Tissington Trail. Follow the Trail northwards, crossing Bentley Brook, where there was once a viaduct, then a girder bridge over Spend Lane. About a mile/1.6km further on, pass under a bridge

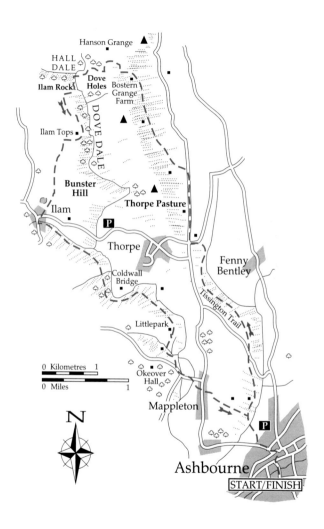

Hanson Grange

HALL DALE

Dove Holes

Ilam Rock

Bostern Grange Farm

DOVE DALE

Ilam Tops

Bunster Hill

Thorpe Pasture

Ilam

P

Thorpe

Fenny Bentley

Coldwall Bridge

Tissington Trail

Littlepark

0 Kilometres 1

0 Miles 1

Okeover Hall

N

Mappleton

P

Ashbourne

START/FINISH

to reach the site of Thorpe Cloud station. Go left, and at the Dog and Partridge turn right, going straight ahead at the next junction, up a narrow lane. Climb steadily, with Thorpe Cloud coming into view on the left, soon entering Thorpe Pastures, owned by the National Trust.

The lane soon leaves the open pastures, becoming walled again. At the footpath signs, go left, following the obvious track. Beyond the dip, go right, through a stile. Pass through the gateway just to the left. Head for a marker post, skirting to the right of another little quarry to a stile. Pass a small plantation on the left and a lime kiln built into the hillside. Here the path leaves the wall and takes off across fields. The stiles are mostly waymarked with posts.

Descend towards Bostern Grange, passing across the end of a dry valley running left towards Dovedale. Go to a stile in the corner of the wall, then follow the wall round the shoulder of the right-hand hill to Bostern Grange Farm. Skirt to the right of the buildings to a gate and turn left. Proceed up through a pathless meadow to a stile in the corner. Now descending, the path comes to a stile by a gate. Go over, and immediately right, beside the wall.

Head across a rough field towards Hanson Grange. At the signpost, turn left, dropping down into Nabs Dale, over limestone rubble, passing a small cave on the right. Soon the main Dovedale path is reached. Go left here, beside the lovely Dove as it chatters over fish weirs.

On the left are the Dove Holes, readily accessible

from the path. Continue downstream, soon reaching spectacular Ilam Rock.

A footbridge leads across to the base of the rock. Turn right, following the Staffordshire bank for about 150yds/m until the path begins to swing away from the river. An easily missed waymarker post points left, to Ilam. Follow this steep path up a series of zigzags.

At the top of the hill keep left where the path forks, continuing along the edge of the wood. Soon a couple of ladder stiles take the path out on to an upland meadow. A broad track leads past some rocky outcrops to Air Cottage Farm.

There is a grand view down into the dale and a spectacular view to the south over Thorpe Cloud to the Trent valley.

Skirt to the left of the farm buildings. then through a stile on the right. Cross a small paddock and go left along a track for about 200yds/m, almost to Ilam Tops Farm. Then go left, before the gate, along the avenue of trees.

Pass the large barn and go through the gateway ahead, following the right-hand wall, to a stile and National Trust sign at Bunster Hill. The right of way follows the wall on the western side of Bunster, skirting the base of the hill to a small signposted gate and the road.

Turn right to Ilam Cross. Turn left and cross the Manifold, then left again along the riverside path. After a series of stiles, bear away to the right, following the waymarks uphill through scrub before coming into open pasture. The path makes a bee-line for the right-hand end of Coldwall Bridge, crossing a culverted stream en route.

Coldwall Bridge is an early turnpike structure, built to serve the needs of the Staffordshire pottery industry.

Skirt round the easternmost end of the bridge, before dropping down to river level again. Follow a broad stony track by the river and through a wood. Where the track emerges from the wood, leave the riverbank and cut across a field, making for the bottom of Little Peg's Wood. The river crowds in from the left, squeezing the track against the woodland. Just beyond a gate the track forks. Bear right through the trees, soon emerging into fields. Go straight on, passing to the right of Littlepark Farm before turning left and dropping to a sign-posted stile on to the farm access.

Here go right. Follow the track for about 200yds/m, to a stile half hidden in the left-hand hedge. Bear right across the field along an obvious path, soon coming close to the Dove again. The river swings away at the weir and the path follows the mill race, making for the right of the buildings.

Join a track on to the road, opposite the entrance to Okeover Park. Go left, crossing the fine Okeover Bridge, which spans the Dove, taking the walk back into Derbyshire. Just beyond the bridge, cut across the field on the right to emerge opposite the pub.

Go past the pub and the row of cottages, then turn

left. Follow the path along the front of the cottages into fields. Bear right, heading up the field to a stile to the right of the gate.

Continue climbing, bearing left, then crossing a series of fields, and the access track to Callow Top Farm. Go straight on, through another stile, with Ashbourne in view to the right, before dropping steeply down through more fields to reach the Tissington Trail via a flight of steps. Turn right for Ashbourne and Mappleton Lane car park.

14 Buxton to Earl Sterndale

A grand walk in the unfrequented country of the Upper Dove, finishing with the spectacular reef "mountains" of Parkhouse and Chrome Hills. This walk necessitates a bus ride from Earl Sterndale to Buxton and can be combined with walk 15 to give a good day's walking.

Distance:
6 ¾ miles/11km
Height gain:
1,300ft/400m
Walking time:
4 hours
Start:
Buxton Market Place. GR058733. Plenty of parking in town.
Finish:
Earl Sterndale (Quiet Woman) GR090670. Roadside parking in village.
Type of walk:
Field paths and old packhorse trails, with gentle climbing.
Public transport:
Daily buses to Buxton from Sheffield, Bakewell, Nottingham, Derby, Matlock, London, Leek, the Potteries, Stockport and Manchester. Daily trains from Blackpool, Preston, Manchester and Stockport. Daily buses to Earl Sterndale from Buxton and Hartington.

From the Market Place, go south down the A515, passing the traffic lights by the London Road pub. About 450yds/m beyond the lights, turn right along Fern Road. Follow the lane through parkland to a

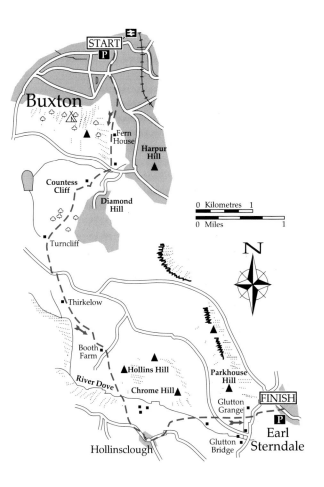

cattle grid, then over a stile on the right. Follow the left-hand wall, parallel the lane. Continue through a series of stiles, soon passing Fern House stables and reaching a walled track. At the end of the track continue alongside the trees. Where the wall swings left, go straight ahead, over the brow of the hill, where a view of Harpur Hill materialises. Descend to cross a track and bear slightly right to a stile on to the Ladmanlow road. Go left to the bottom of the dip, then go right, on to a track. Follow the stream for a short distance before zigzagging up to Countess Cliff Farm. A more direct path cuts off the zigzags, leading to the farm gate.

The tower on the horizon is Solomon's Temple. The complex of buildings to the left is the Harpur Hill industrial estate, which started life as a wartime store and became the mines research station.

Beyond the farmyard there is a stile on the left, into fields. Bear right, down and across a series of fields to a prominently waymarked stile leading into the research station grounds.

The prominent embankment on the left marks the course of the former Cromford and High Peak Railway. Opened in the 1830s and closed in the 1960s, it is now a road.

Follow the waymarks until a tarred lane is reached by a water tank. Follow the lane, soon crossing the former railway and reaching Turncliff. Follow the signposted lane to the left. This ends at a turning circle, by the headwaters of the River Wye. Go past the "sentry" box, up the grass to the right of the tall trees, making for a ladder stile on the horizon. At the stile, go left along the road, passing over the cattle grid and then going right, along a track at the base of Thirkelow Rocks which rise to the left. The road marks the watershed between the Wye and Dove.

Continue past Thirkelow, with limestone hills to the left and shales/grits on the opposite site of the stream. The track keeps high above the stream then swings away to the left, descending to cross a small brook before following the broad green path up the nose of land between two streams, almost to Booth Farm. Bear left round a marshy area to a stile in the wall. The path clips the field corner to a stile by a bath, then heads away from the farm to a lane. Go right, skirting to the left of the farm, following the sign to Fough.

The hillside to the left is Hollin, one of the spectacular group that guards the northern end of Dovedale. From this angle it is tame.

Continue past Fough, keeping right at the way-marked fork, imperceptibly moving into the main valley of the Dove and descending gradually. The broad green track swings round the end of Hollin Hill, suddenly revealing Chrome and Parkhouse Hills in all their serrated glory.

Where the track continues to Hollins Farm, the path is waymarked to the right. Descend steeply to cross the Dove on a lovely little packhorse bridge, thus entering Staffordshire. Follow the path up through the field, to the Hollinsclough road.

Turn left at Hollinsclough chapel, following the road past the little school. About 450yds/m from the chapel, where the road begins to bend right, go left along a rough lane. Follow this to a T-junction, bearing right to a ford and footbridge over the Dove and back into Derbyshire.

Continue along the track skirting Stannery Farm to reach the Dowel Dale road. Go along the road, soon bearing left towards a yellow stone. An obvious path skirts the base of Parkhouse Hill, passing through a number of bright yellow painted stiles to the road. Go straight across, bearing left up the hillside, still following yellow stiles or painted boulders. A sharp climb soon reaches the shoulder of Hitter Hill. The tower of Earl Sterndale church comes into view, forming a good marker for the route into the village. A stile by a gate leads out on to the road, just opposite the bus stop. The village green and the Quiet Woman pub lie just to the right.

15 Earl Sterndale to Hartington

A superb descent into Dovedale leads to easy riverside paths as far as Crowdecote. Then the less frequented Staffordshire side of the valley is followed through Upper and Under Whittle almost to Sheen before a final canter down to Hartington. This walk can be combined with walk 14 to give a good day's outing. Both require the use of the local bus at the start or end of the day.

Distance:
5$\frac{1}{4}$ miles/9km
Height gain:
570ft/175m
Walking time:
3 hours
Start:
Earl Sterndale (Quiet Woman) GR090670. Roadside parking.
Finish:
Hartington Square. Roadside and pay/display in village.
Type of walk:
Delightfully easy dale or lane walking, but with two steep descents and one climb.
Public transport:
Earl Sterndale has daily buses from Hartington and Buxton. Hartington has daily buses from Buxton and Earl Sterndale, with infrequent services from Ashbourne and Leek. Additional seasonal services.

From the Quiet Woman go left on the signposted path between the pub and barn. Follow the signs for Crowdecote, soon reaching open fields. Go

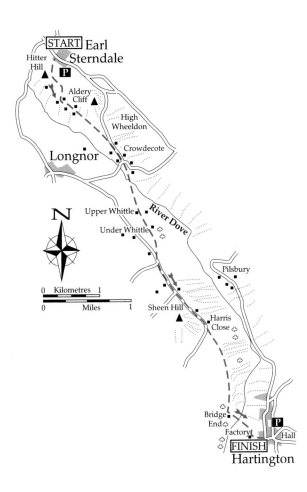

START Earl Sterndale

Hitter Hill

Aldery Cliff

High Wheeldon

Longnor

Crowdecote

River Dove

Upper Whittle

Under Whittle

N

Pilsbury

0 Kilometres 1
0 Miles 1

Sheen Hill

Harris Close

Bridge End

Factory

FINISH Hartington

Hall

uphill alongside the wall, soon reaching a stile almost on the top of Hitter Hill. Bear left alongside the wall, over the brow of the hill, where suddenly a view of Dovedale is revealed, with Sheen Hill beyond. Continue to follow the wall until it does a left and right kink.

Fork right, going steeply downhill to join the main Dovedale path at Underhill. Go left here. Enjoy an easy 600yds/m stroll along this lovely valley, passing Underhill Farm on the right. Just beyond the farm the track swings left into a broad green lane.

This green lane marks one of the former drove road crossing points of the Dove. To the right lies Beggars' Bridge and the road to Longnor. To the left the old road passes through the cleft between Aldery Cliff and High Wheeldon to gain the limestone plateau.

Go straight on along the signposted footpath, soon passing Meadow Farm and joining the road to Crowdecote about 100yds/m before the village. Go through the village, passing the Packhorse on the left and then bearing left at Toll Bar cottage.

Bear right where the lane forks, following the signs to Sheen and Pilsbury. At Bridge End Farm, just before the Permastore silo, go right, down to the ford and footbridge over the Dove, into Staffordshire. Bear left at the multiple-armed signpost, following the sign to Sheen.

This path is well waymarked. Initially it stays fairly close to the river, but after crossing a tributary stream it tends uphill, making for Upper Whittle

Farm. Pass through the field below Upper Whittle to join a track. Go left here, soon approaching a range of ruined buildings. Pass to the right of the ruins, heading up across the hillside to an obvious waymark. The right of way follows a muddy and tortuous course round a recently constructed pond before joining a track.

Follow the track for a short distance until it swings right at a hairpin bend. The signposted path goes straight ahead, with good views down into Dovedale and to Pilsbury Castle. The path meanders along the hillside, soon reaching Under Whittle. Follow the access track up the hillside to the road and go left.

A mile/1.6km of road walking now follows. Half way along, look out for the drove road coming up from Pilsbury on the left. As Sheen Hill is left behind, Sheen church comes into view to the right and the hills around Wetton and the Manifold.

At Harris Close Farm go left at the signposted footpath, then turn right and squeeze between the right-hand barn and the wall to emerge in open fields. Follow the right-hand wall through a series of fields until suddenly Hartington comes into view ahead and below. Skirt an area of landslip, a sure sign that this side of the valley is shale, passing through a belt of pines. The path is waymarked steeply down to the left to join a farm track at an awkward stile. Go right briefly before turning off the track at a signpost. The obvious path soon reaches a bridge over the Dove, passing back into Derbyshire again.

Bear right now, across the fields, through a series of stiles, making for the cheese factory. The path soon passes into a new plantation, skirting to the left of the buildings, before emerging on the road. The village centre lies just to the left, with an attractive array of shops, cafes and pubs.

16 Hartington and Alstonefield

A busy start through Hartington and Berresford Dale leads into quiet Narrow Dale. Alstonefield is the next port of call and then comes the steep descent into Wolfscote Dale. A grand path is followed by a diversion up Biggin Dale and then over the top of the limestone plateau for a return to Hartington.

Distance:
9 miles/14km
Height gain:
1,090ft/335m
Walking time:
5 hours
Start/Finish:
Hartington Square.
GR128604. Roadside
and pay/display
parking in village.
Type of walk:
Easy riverside paths

and little-used field
paths, plus old
packhorse trails. One
very steep descent.
Public transport:
Hartington has daily
bus services from
Buxton. Less frequent
services from
Ashbourne and Leek.
Additional seasonal
services operate.

From the square go along the Warslow road. At the toilets, go left along the path signposted Dovedale. The path soon reaches and crosses a narrow green lane, then continues towards Berresford Dale.

This is "Compleat Angler" country and the prominent tower seen ahead is part of the now demolished Berresford Hall, home of Charles Cotton. To the right there is a broad

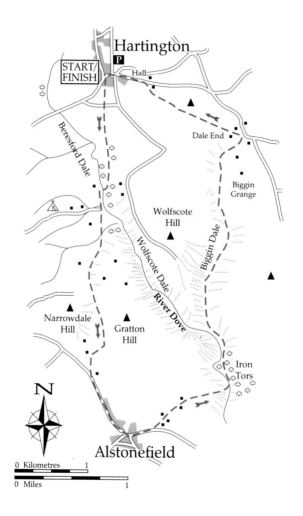

view across both the Dove and Manifold valleys, which here are divided by a very low ridge. The prominent hills that mark the most spectacular part of the Manifold are clearly seen.

The path soon passes through a gateway, bearing left to a stile in the bottom of the field. Pass along the base of a limestone knoll, soon entering the woodland of Berresford Dale, with the Fishing Temple of Berresford Hall on the right. This is real limestone dale scenery, with rocky crags and the lovely River Dove. Cross the bridge and continue along the dale, passing Pikes Pool with its spire of rock. Ignore the next footbridge and continue ahead to Berresford Lane. Go right, but in about 100yds/m, go left through a stile on to a track.

The scenery has subtly changed in this short distance. To the left is the limestone dale, whilst to the right the broad valley betrays the presence of shale.

Follow the broad track which soon becomes a rough, walled lane, making for Narrowdale Farm. To the left lies the constrained entrance to Narrow Dale. Where the lane turns to the right, pass through a gate on the left, entering the dale. Follow the path up the dale bottom, which has scarcely sufficient width at first but soon broadens.

There is a good view back, with the northern Dovedale hills framed in the portals of Narrow Dale.

Climb to the head of Narrow Dale. At the gate there is no exit so go right, to a stile into a narrow lane. Follow the lane to the right then go left through a stile signposted to Alstonefield. Bear right to the corner of the clump of trees, then head diagonally across to reach a stile and the road. Go left for Alstonefield.

Hopedale can be seen ahead and to the right, whilst the prominent hill on the right is Steeplow. Wetton village can be seen further to the right, whilst further away still the spire of Grindon church can just be discerned.

Bear left at the Y-junction, then left again at the T-junction to the centre of the village. Pass the village green and the George Inn on the right, then the former chapel on the left, leaving the village behind. At the second footpath sign on the left, about 400yds/m from the village green, go left along a walled green lane.

The prominent knoll on the far side of Dovedale is Mootlow, but there is little sense of the proximity of Dovedale until the lane does a sharp right and left turn and the valley comes into view. Coldeaton Dale can be seen running east, whilst Biggin Dale flows away north-east.

The lane goes steadily downhill, but still the arrival at the top of the descent to Coldeaton Bridge comes as a shock. The lane ends abruptly at Gipsey Bank. Bear right, descending the steep zig-zags to the bridge. Cross the Dove into Derbyshire and go left along the obvious path, close to the river.

The rocky outcrops of Iron Tors are hidden in the trees to the right. A disused hydraulic ram on the right once supplied water from the Dove to farms on the top of the plateau. About 200yds/m further on there is a cave on the right. At the junction of Wolfscote Dale and Biggin Dale, turn right. Biggin Dale is a dramatic dry valley. In about 400yds/m the path passes another cave on the right and soon reaches the boundary of the National Nature Reserve.

As the path rounds a corner of the dale, Biggin Grange comes into view on top of the hill. Where the dale forks, a footpath sign points to Hartington. Skirt a dewpond and go left, through a gate, descending to the dale bottom before bearing right. After 300yds/m, another signpost points to Hartington, but this time go straight on, up the dale, over a stile signed to Biggin. Soon the path passes another dewpond on the left, closely followed by Biggin sewage works. Follow the access track up to the road and there go left. Biggin village lies just to the right. About 100yds/m along the road, by Dale End House, bear left along a rough green lane.

The lane is paved with limestone slabs in places. At the Y-junction keep right, going straight ahead at the T-junction about 50yds/m further on. Another 350yds/m brings the lane to the top of the hill and a tremendous view opens up, taking in all the upper reaches of Dovedale and the Manifold. Continue down the lane, towards Hartington. Just past the barn on the left, go left over a signposted stile into fields, bearing right alongside the wall. Pass through a gateway and then go straight ahead to another gateway to the left of the trees. Now go right to a third (signposted) gate, on to a road, close to the YHA at Hartington Hall. Go left along the road, soon reaching the square.

17 Hulme End and Manifold Valley

The first half of the walk lies along the old Manifold Valley railway route, in spectacular limestone scenery. The highlight is an optional visit to Thor's Cave, perched high above the valley. There follows a delightful stroll through Wetton and Back of Ecton on peaceful paths, to Hulme End.

Distance:
7½ miles/13km
Height gain:
950ft/290m
Walking time:
4 hours 15 minutes
Start/Finish:
Manifold Valley Visitor Centre, Hulme End. GR103593. Pay/display parking at visitor centre.
Type of walk:
Generally easy, on surfaced or obvious tracks, but some very muddy stretches and one optional steep, exposed ascent.
Public transport:
Hulme End has daily bus services from Hartington and Buxton. Less frequent services to Ashbourne and Leek. Additional seasonal services operate.

The first few miles of this walk lie along the trackbed of the former Manifold Valley railway. The start of the walk is the former terminus of the line. If time permits, call in at the visitor centre, in the station buildings. The line opened in 1904 and closed in 1934.

Go south along the trackbed, in a broad shale valley. After 500yds/m, the valley narrows appreciably and the railway, river and road are crowded together. Ecton Hill rises to the left, and the land rises equally steeply to the right. Pass over the River Manifold on one of the numerous bridges. The valley soon becomes even more constrained. About 15 minutes after leaving Hulme End, pass over the lane coming down from Warslow and enter Ecton.

There seems to be little to generate any railway business here, but a glance at the hillside on the left will show the scars of mineral working. Ecton Hill is riddled with shafts and adits from centuries of copper mining. The opening of the railway was expected to lead to the mines re-opening, but this did not materialise. Instead, a creamery was built, so the mainstay of traffic was milk. The copper-roofed building on the hillside on the left was the mine manager's house.

Pass through the wide open space once occupied by the station, before continuing along the track. A further 15 minutes gentle stroll brings the walker to Butterton station. Leave the line via the footpath on the left, crossing a footbridge over Warslow Brook, cutting across to a stile, just to the right of the fine arched road bridge, that spans the Manifold. Cross the river and turn right just beyond the bridge, passing through a gate on to a narrow lane.

Until the railway tunnel was converted into a proper road in the 1950s, this lane was the only vehicular access into the valley. Now it is virtually unused. Soon there is a fine view across to Swainsley Hall, with the Manifold

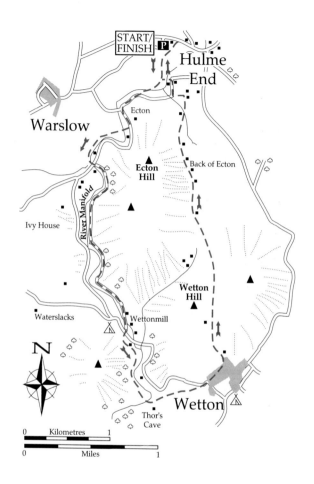

sweeping round and over a series of fish weirs. The owner of Swainsley Hall was a railway shareholder, but he insisted that the line should not spoil his view, but should tunnel through the hillside instead.

The lane soon begins to rise away from the river, soon passing a cave on the left, probably an old copper working. The drop to the river is quite precipitous in places. Soon the lane reaches Dale Farm, and joins another road. Turn right, following the road round the knoll to Wetton Mill, an oasis, serving food and drink to visitors. It is now in the ownership of the National Trust, along with large tracts of land in the Manifold and Dove valleys.

Cross the bridge and the former railway, turning left at the T-junction immediately beyond. Pass through the shallow ford, and continue into the narrowing valley, with limestone crags on either side. Cross the fine single-arched Darfar Bridge, to reach the former level crossing where the road quits the valley, heading up to Wetton.

In summer the river sinks into pot holes near Wetton Mill and only re-emerges near Ilam. In winter there can be a mighty flow, however, even amounting to flood proportions.

Continue down the former railway, which here is traffic free. The track swings round a couple more bends, until suddenly Thor's Cave comes into view.

This is one of the most dramatic features in the whole of the Peak. It is seemingly inaccessible, high above the valley and at the base of towering cliffs.

Where the line swings to the right, go left to a bridge over the Manifold. Beyond the bridge the path quickly forks. The route to the right is not a right of way and is both steep and slippery. Carry straight on, through the trees and scrub, until a waymark post is reached in about 325yds/m. (The option to visit Thor's Cave starts here, up the path to the right. It is steep but it leads unerringly to the cave. There is a considerable feeling of exposure on the final part of this ascent). The main route carries on up the dale, through scrub, out into open fields to the road near Wetton.

Keep straight on at the T-junction, pass the squat little church on the right and then, where the road swings right, go left, up a farm track, following the signs to Back of Ecton up the rough lane. The lane rises steadily, passing a grass-covered reservoir and a small, partly filled-in quarry working, to a way-marked stile. The path rises across the field to another stile where there is a National Trust sign. Go straight on across the pathless hillside, making for the bottom right of Wetton Hill, seen ahead. A path soon materialises, descending on slippery limestone to a stile. Go diagonally right to a stile which stands right on the col between the west and east summits of Wetton Hill.

Descend the broad path by the wall with Ecton Hill ahead. Where the wall bends to the left, go straight ahead on a broad green path, passing a solitary standing stone. A shallow valley goes off to the left but the path continues ahead. Cross a culverted stream, but then wade along another watercourse to a stile in the corner of the field. Bear left, ascending to a stile by the line of trees. Cross the vegetation-choked green lane, go through the gap in the wall and turn right, to a tarred lane, by Cantrell's House Farm.

Continue along the road until it swings to the right by a barn. A track goes off to the left here, through a gate, and the footpath required by this walk should also leave the road here and then go right, just before the gate. There is no stile and the fence is difficult to negotiate. Once in the field, bear right, heading to a stile in the middle of the far wall. Bear right again, passing through a line of trees, heading towards East Ecton Farm.

Drop down to the right of the first barn to a concrete track, following this down to the lane. Follow the lane for about 500yds/m, turning right at the T-junction near the telephone box. After 325yds/m, when Westside Mill is reached, go between the buildings, bearing left through a gateway, to a footbridge over the Manifold. Bear right, soon leaving the riverbank, heading across the meadows to reach the former railway again. Turn right here for the final 325yds/m back to Hulme End.

18 Monyash and High Wheeldon

A delightful walk over the limestone plateau leads to the superb viewpoint of High Wheeldon. A steep descent past Aldery Cliff takes the walker into the Dove Valley and to Crowdecote. Then along the Dove valley past Pilsbury Castle and up on to the plateau again, before a return to Monyash.

Distance:
9½ miles/16km
Height gain:
1,710ft/523m
Walking time:
5½ hours
Start/Finish:
Monyash Square. GR150665. Limited roadside parking in village. Small car park on the Flagg road.
Type of walk:
Easy tracks and field paths across the plateau and along Dovedale. One steep ascent/descent.
Public transport:
Monyash has Monday to Saturday bus services to Buxton.

Go along the Flagg road, bearing left at the far end of the car park through a small gate. Head across the field to the left of the cottage. Go left, swinging to the right round the end of the cottages before bearing left, across a field, passing through a gap in the wall. Left again, following the path through a series of stiles, to a walled track. Here go right. The track bends to the left almost at once and begins a gentle climb. Where the track forks, keep right. After about 350yds/m, go sharp left by a barn.

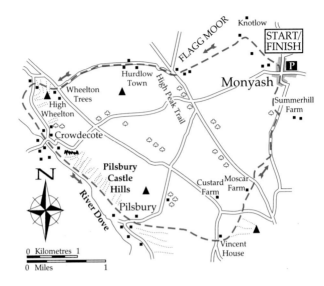

Just north of the barn were the Knotlow lead mines, which were served by these various tracks and paths. To the right, the village of Flagg can clearly be seen. The prominent hill is Chelmorton Low.

After an almost straight mile/1.6km, the track reaches the A515 at the Bull i't'Thorn. Go right here for about 200yds/m, until almost opposite the turning to Flagg. Go left over the signposted stile and follow the wall to another signposted stile, there going right. Bear left, making for the bridge under the High Peak Trail.

The trail was formerly part of the Buxton to Ashbourne railway, a relative newcomer by railway standards, only being completed in the closing years of the 19th century. However, this section is much older, for it was constructed in 1869 to replace the Hurdlow incline on the even earlier (1830s) Cromford and High Peak Railway.

Go under the bridge and bear right, soon following the wall on the right to the road. Go right here, passing through Hurdlow. On the left can be seen the dry-stone embankment of the original 1830s line of the Cromford and High Peak Railway. The road tops the first rise out of Hurdlow and the tip of High Wheeldon hill can be seen ahead. A slight dip and another rise widens the view still further.

The hills at the northern end of the Dove valley are clearly seen, with the reef knolls, Hollin, Parkhouse and Chrome, being particularly noticeable. Southwards the view encompasses much of the limestone plateau, and gritstone-capped Sheen Hill.

The lane drops to a junction, where a stile leads down to a gate by a National Trust sign. A short, steep ascent follows to the summit of High Wheeldon.

The view is hidden until the last moment, but is worth the wait. The Upper Dove is spread out below like a map. The reef hills are proudly displayed to the north, along with Axe Edge Moor. West and south are the hills of the Staffordshire moorlands, whilst south-east and east is the rolling countryside of the White Peak.

Descend High Wheeldon along the steep northwest ridge, passing the gated entrance to Fox Hole Cave on the right. Further descent is soon barred by a wall. Skirt to the right until the wall ceases before picking a way down to the stile and road at the foot of Aldery Cliff, a well-known climbing venue. Go left until the road forks, then bear right. The lane rapidly degenerates into a grassy track. About 250yds/m from the junction, go left at a crossing of paths, soon passing Meadow Farm and joining the road to Crowdecote about 100yds/m before the village.

Pass the Packhorse pub and bear left at Toll Bar cottage, bearing right where the lane forks, following the signs to Sheen and Pilsbury. Skirt to the right of Bridge End Farm along a track, and into a walled lane. This runs for about 250yds/m before entering a field. A well-blazed path leads down the valley, with the Dove to the right, soon reaching a gateway at the base of Pilsbury Castle Hill and then swinging up and left to skirt the knoll of limestone.

Pilsbury Castle was a motte and bailey construction, making use of an existing limestone outcrop. It is best seen from a vantage point a little further on in the walk, but it is worth the short deviation into the site itself.

Just past the limestone buttress on the right, go over a stile on the left, keeping left where the path forks. Climb steadily, glancing back for views of Pilsbury Castle. Keep alongside the wall on a distinct waymarked path, until a stile is reached in the corner of the field. Do not bear right to join the road. Carry straight on through two fields heading to the right of the barn, and cross the road to a large pointed stone gatepost. Keep straight on at the signposted stile and head up the middle of the shallow valley, soon passing through a gateway and skirting a large pond.

Follow the path as it swings to the right, following a line of pylons and heading towards the cluster of tin sheds and a waymarked stile. Head slightly uphill towards an outcrop of stones, soon cresting the rise, to disclose Parsley Hay. An indistinct path drops straight down the hillside to Vincent House Farm and the road. Go through the farmyard on to a track leading up the hillside, passing the silica sand pits. Pass through the gateway, and where the track bears away to the right, carry straight on to a waymarked stile. Follow the left-hand wall, soon cresting the rise disclosing a view to the left to High Wheeldon. Still following the wall, descend through fields to the road, close to Darley Farm.

Go through the farmyard, using the waymarked middle gate, then following the wall on the right. Go up and over the embankment of the Trail into fields again. Go up the field to a stile, then follow the wall on the left to a gate, leading into the paddock in front of Moscar Farm. In the paddock bear right to a signposted stile, continuing straight ahead, skirting to the right of the farm and following a wall on the left to reach the A515.

Go left for about 50yds/m then right at a signposted stile, back into fields. Bear left to a well hidden stile to the right of two trees. Keep straight on to a stile to the right of an electricity pylon. Make for the left-hand edge of the plantation and pass through a stile in the middle of the cross wall, continuing along the same alignment to a stile in the left-hand wall. Diagonally across this field to a stile by a bush, then go right to the road. Turn left along the road, passing Highlow Farm, before swinging to the right.

About 500yds/m beyond the bend, a steel gate on the left leads into a green lane. Where the lane narrows, there is a gate on the right and a squeeze stile between gatepost and wall. Bear left, over the outcrops of rock to a stile in the cross wall. Go left to a gateway and then right by the wall. A gate leads into a vegetation-choked green lane, which swings right and soon widens into a broad green track, weaving through clumps of nettles.

Pass into a driveway between two buildings, soon reaching the road near Monyash Mere. Go left for the short trot back to the square.

19 Waterhouses and Onecote

The walk includes two contrasting sections of the Hamps valley. The first, from Waterhouses to Onecote, is very quiet, in fine shale/gritstone scenery. The second is the grand limestone valley traversed by the popular Manifold/Hamps track. The link over Grindon Moor is little walked, but with fine views.

Distance:
10½ miles/17 km
Height gain:
1,235 ft/380m
Walking time:
6 hours
Start/Finish:
Waterhouses, Old Crown Inn. GR084502.
Pay/display parking at the old station. GR085501
Type of walk:
Quiet valley and hill walking on little-used field paths, then easy tracks along the lower Hamps valley. One awkward river crossing.

Public transport:
Waterhouses has daily buses from Manchester, Stockport, Macclesfield, Leek, Ashbourne and Derby. Less frequent services run to Cheadle and the Potteries.

Go along the A523 towards Leek, crossing the River Hamps. Opposite the war memorial a narrow path passes round the back of the Old Beams Hotel, crossing the drive to Stonesteads and soon reaching the sports club car park. Go along Port-

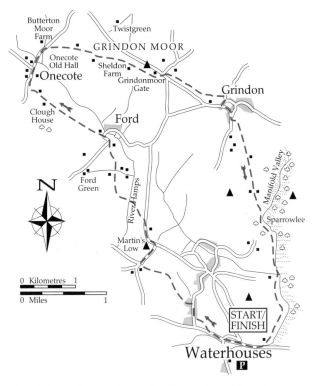

land Way, then right at the T-junction. After about 300yds/m, turn left up Cross Lane, which soon degenerates to a rough track.

The curiously-shaped hill to the left is part of Cauldon Low quarry which provided stone for the Thames barrier.

Climb gently to Waterfall Cross, going right and soon reaching a T-junction. Go left, passing Martinslow trig point on the left and Martinslow Farm on the right. About 200yds/m beyond the farm go left at a signposted stile, to the little brick barn. Pass to the right of it, making a beeline for Stonyslack Farm, on the far side of the valley. Go through a derelict fence, bearing left into the trees, crossing a bridge, and re-entering fields.

Turn left to a stile leading on to a steep, hawthorn-clad bank. Bear right, down through the thorns, looking out for the stepping stones across the river, as the path bypasses them. Cross the stepping stones, which can be quite tricky, especially if the river is in spate.

Bear right up the field to a stile, heading to the right of the barn and left of Stoneyslack Farm house, to a gate. Go into the farm yard, bearing left and then right, passing round another barn to a stile. Cross a rough field, bearing left to the three trees at the wall corner. Turn left at a gap in the fence by the three trees, following the wall up to a stile. Turn right to Sycamore Lodge. Skirt left of the house, then bear right to locate a stile on the left.

Go straight across the field to a stile. Follow the left-hand wall, going through the gateway at the far end of the field, bearing left at this point to follow the fence through a couple more fields to Ford Farm. Keep right of the first corrugated iron barn, entering the farmyard.

Turn right in the farmyard to reach a lane. In about 100yds/m turn right at a T-junction, descending to the delightful hamlet of Ford. Just before the bridge, turn left along another lane paralleling the river, ascending to Banktop Farm.

Go right, following the sign to Bullclough, passing through the farmyard and exiting by the left-hand gateway. Bear left, making for the right-hand end of the clump of trees. Skirt the trees over rough ground, to pick up an indistinct track. Follow the track through a series of fields, always keeping alongside the left-hand boundary.

A gated track diverges left at a boggy patch, but go straight on, heading across the mid-field to a sign-post, passing Bull Clough Farm on the left. At the signpost go straight on, crossing a bridge, then climbing to a stile into the grounds of Field House. Skirt to the left of the garden, soon joining the driveway. Go left, following the drive to Onecote.

Turn right at the road, through the village, passing over the Hamps and continuing as far as the right-hand bend, and the driveway leading to Onecote Old Hall. Go right here, then immediately left, over a stile. Bear right, heading up the slope, passing to the left of the buildings to a stile. Continue uphill alongside a steep-sided little valley. Pass an old barn, continuing up alongside the fence, bearing gently to the right, with fine views down the Hamps towards Cauldon Low.

Skirt the tip of Grindon Moor to a stile, then head past the solitary thorn. Continue on the same alignment, bearing right at the next stile, soon crossing the track from Mount Pleasant Farm. A sketchy path runs alongside the wall, After two sets of duckboards, the path passes through a stile, closely followed by another stile, on the right. Go through this and turn left, following the wall. Traverse a couple more fields, heading towards Sheldon Farm.

The path goes straight across the field, not heading for the obvious gate, but for a hidden stile to the right. Skirt to the left of the silage clamp, crossing the farm access to reach a signposted stile. Keep left of the disintegrating barn to a signposted stile. Carry straight on, roughly parallel with the road, making for the right of the house. Cross the access track to Grindonmoor Gate Farm, into a tiny field.

There is an excellent view over the limestone hills of the Manifold and Hamps valleys, as well as north towards Warslow.

A step stile leads on to the road. Go over a stile almost opposite, turning right once in the field, proceeding more or less parallel to the road, to a stile. Bear right, almost rejoining the road again, but at the far end of the field, there is a stile on the right, into a very narrow field. Turn left and follow the wall, with Grindon spire straight ahead. The field soon broadens and the path passes through a gap in a tumble-down wall. Cross a couple of rough fields. A straight course for the church is not possible, so head for the black hut instead, bearing left at the wall corner.

There is a grand view over to Wetton and Alstonefield, with the back of Thor's Cave clearly visible and tree-crowned Moot Low very prominent.

Now make a beeline for the church, to reach the picnic site in Grindon village. Turn right along the lane, continuing past the pond and the village green, with the rindle stone to the left. Keep right at the junction, then left at the triangle, soon reaching the Cavalier. Pass in front of the pub with the main road bearing away to the left. About 50yds/m from the pub, a narrow, walled track goes left, soon swinging to the right, passing the front of Green Farm Cottages. Another track joins from the left. The lane rises slowly, passing a derelict barn on the left and topping the rise before entering open fields, where there is a fine view of the Hamps valley below.

Descend into Deepdale. At the signpost bear right, descending more steeply, to a gate in the bottom of the dale, before climbing to the left to the uninhabited farm. Three gates take the track through the farmyard onto a roughly-metalled lane. Where the lane bears right, go straight ahead through a signposted bridlegate, down alongside the wall, following a line of trees. Pass through another bridlegate into a larger field, skirting to the right of the barn. Continue ahead through a gap in the far hedge and wall, across the next field to a third bridlegate. Still descending, cross the next field, leaving it by a fourth bridlegate. Continue alongside the fence, soon locating another gate. Descend quite sharply, through a thicket, to reach another gate into open fields, just above the Hamps-Manifold track.

Keep along the top of the field, soon entering a wood. Descend steadily to the valley bottom, there joining the Hamps track. Lee House Farm cafe at Sparrowlee lies just to the left.

The Hamps is usually dry, for it is one of those disappearing rivers so characteristic of limestone country. The Hamps describes a large U between Ford and Beeston Tor and here it should be flowing north.

Turn right at the track, easy going along a surfaced path, soon crossing the last of the bridges and reaching the A523. Go right here, along the road. After about 300yds/m, look to the right, for here the Hamps is a living river, but at this point it vanishes. A fair stream runs in from the left, into a deep pool. Only a trickle emerges to the right and this quickly sinks into the limestone bed.

A flight of steps on the left of the A523 leads up into the car park. Bus users should follow the road a little further to The Old Crown.

The Limestone Plateau

The limestone plateau is bounded on the east by the Derwent and on the west by the Dove. In between is the heart of the White Peak, rarely exceeding 1,000ft/300m. There are no dramatic hills but numerous little villages and miles of dry-stone walls, probably the best-known feature of the area.

A geographer would describe the area as a dissected plateau, for what the area lacks in height it makes up for in depth. It is scored by many deeply cut valleys, the Derbyshire Dales. Some of these are famous names, Lathkill, Monsal and Millers Dales to name but three. Others are less well-known. Who could pinpoint Silly Dale, Rowdale or Callinglow Dale? Yet all have one thing in common. They are all water-worn, steep-sided valleys, carved out of the limestone at a time when the water table was much higher and when there was a much wetter climate. Many of the dales are now dry or have only seasonal rivers after exceptionally heavy rain. Others have that wonderful blend of water, tree and rock that is so attractive.

On the plateau itself are the remains of earlier habitation and industry. The landscape is pock-marked with holes and hillocks, remnants of centuries of lead mining, with a proven history back to Roman times. The study of the history of lead mining, its legislation and customs is fascinating and an important background to walking and understanding the White Peak. Some of the key lead mining sites are visited by these walks. However, lead mine shafts and adits are dangerous, not to be entered without specialist equipment and knowledge.

The villages of the plateau often have a well dressing tradition, a custom almost unique to Derbyshire. The tradition goes back to pagan times when sources of pure water were worshipped. Like all good pagan customs this one was adopted by the Christian church, as witnessed by the number of wells dedicated to St. Anne. Historians also know her as Arne, the Celtic water goddess. However the present day tradition has probably more to do with tourism than religion, for many villages have only re-established their well dressings within living memory.

There is an incomparable network of paths and tracks left by previous inhabitants, giving a varied selection of routes.

20 Bakewell and Magpie Mine

A stiff pull out of Bakewell precedes a stroll over lime-stone pastures to Magpie Mine. From Sheldon the walk descends through Great Shacklow Wood to a walk alongside the river Wye. Next comes Ashford in the Water. The way back to Bakewell follows little-used paths via Churchdale and over Holme Hall Pasture before a final riverbank walk through Scott's Meadows.

Distance:
10¼ miles/16.4 km
Height gain:
1,380ft/425m
Walking time:
5-6 hours
Start/Finish:
Rutland Square, Bakewell. Pay/display parking in town.
Type of walk:
Field paths and *riverside tracks with no steep ascents.*
Public transport:
Daily buses to Bakewell from Castleton, Sheffield, Chesterfield, London, Nottingham, Derby, Matlock, Buxton, Stockport, Manchester, Leek and the Potteries.

Bakewell is the largest town in the Peak District. It has a flourishing cattle and stall market on Mondays. There are eating places and a wide range of accommodation.

Go along Bridge Street to the riverbank and turn right. At the playing field, bear right to the A6. Cross the road, turn left, then right into Holywell. Go to the right of the shops, then bearing left up a footpath between houses. Climb through a tree belt, assisted by steps, until the path levels out, passing the cemetery. Bear left at a kissing gate. Two more stiles and the route is now truly rural. Descend into a little valley, passing to the right of a pond. Once over the stream, bear right along the ascending track. Where it swings away to the left, go straight on, through a stile in the wall. Still rising, bear left to another stile by a hawthorn tree. Continue to climb, to a stile in the top corner of the next field, by the road.

To the right, on the hillside, a series of terraces in the fields beyond the road marks the alignment of the Portway, or Derbygate, an ancient route.

Go left, turning right at the junction by Noton Barn Farm, ascending steadily. The stile on the left, by the telegraph pole, is easily missed. Leave the lane here, bearing right to a stile at the end of the wall. Continue to bear right across the next field to a double stile. Then make a beeline for the large dead tree, soon reaching Over Haddon, near the Lathkill Hotel.

Walk in front of the pub, with a grand view into Lathkill Dale, then bear right where the road forks and pass the old school. Go down the main street, turning right at the far end, passing the car park. At the next junction bear left. In a little over 220yds/m, go over a stile on the right, by a corrugated metal barn. Follow the left-hand wall up the field, turning left at the top to a signposted stile. Bear right, diagonally across the field, making for a large tree, seen on the horizon. Now head towards Mel-

bourne Farm, but at the next stile go sharp right, alongside the wall to a well-hidden stile in the corner. This change of direction is easily missed. Head towards the left-hand end of the tree belt, then make for a solitary tall tree, so reaching the B5055. Turn right, then left, over a stile, following the path up and over the hill, through a series of stiles. After the third stile, the path is signed round the corner of a field for no obvious reason.

This was Magshaw Mine. Originally this was mined for lead in the traditional manner with shafts. The spoil was deposited as close to the shaft top as possible, raising the general ground level considerably. The spoil heaps were subsequently re-worked. The trees on the site indicate the former ground level, for they are perched on little hillocks.

A stile in the right-hand fence leads to a way-marked path across the old workings, signed to Sheldon. The clump of trees to the left crowns Bole Hill. A "bole" was a primitive smelter, which relied on a good supply of local timber and wind.

Waymarked stiles lead the path through a narrow tree belt into fields, then down to the Kirkdale road. Go right briefly, then left, up a narrow green lane into fields, where the impressive remains of Magpie Mine come into view. The path skirts to the right of the mine, passing through a stile near the thorn trees before bearing left to reach the field corner, where a stile leads into the Magpie site, close to the powder house and an adit.

The chimney, "Cornish" engine house and reconstructed horse "gin" are the most prominent features, but there is a wealth of interest here for the industrial archaeologist. The history of Magpie is fascinating. The tale is of money made and lost, of bitter argument and murder, of curses and ghosts. Visit the Peak District Mines Society office on the site, for more information.

Leave the site by a path to the left of the powder house, soon reaching a stile in the wall. (This is not the same stile used to enter the site.) Go straight across to a signposted stile and head almost due north to another lead mine access lane. Go right, following the wall to a gate and entering the maze of tiny fields on the outskirts of Sheldon. Numerous paths lead into the village, but they do not show up well, even on the 1:25,000 map. Head diagonally left to a stile, then across a very narrow field, exiting left by a dewpond and soon reaching the village street. Go right, down the road to the pub.

Almost opposite the pub, a narrow green lane runs down the left-hand side of the churchyard. Beyond the church the lane bends to the left, descending for about 220yds/m until a gate is reached. At this point go right, down a very narrow, overgrown, walled track, finishing at a stile. Follow the wall down into the dale bottom, then through a belt of trees. Climb out of the dale and follow a wall over the brow of the hill to a gate, entering Great Shacklow Wood.

Great Shacklow Wood is a real delight, a mixed deciduous woodland with a carpet of wildflowers in season and full of birdsong.

Descend steeply through the trees. After about 220yds/m go right, down an even steeper flight of steps, to the valley floor footpath. Turn right, soon coming alongside the River Wye.

The powerful stream emerging from the hillside is Magpie Sough Tail, a drainage level dug to unwater Magpie. The 1979 date on the stone arching was the date of reopening. Some years previously a blocked air shaft caused water pressure to build up to such an extent that the blockage was blown clear, bringing about a landslide which covered the sough tail completely.

Continue by the river to Ashford Mill. Pass the tail-race from the mill, soon reaching the Kirkdale road. Turn left to the A6, bearing right towards Bakewell. After about 300yds/m, cross the road and then the Wye at Sheepwash Bridge.

The bridge gets its name from the practice of washing the sheep in the river just downstream of the bridge. Ashford is a lovely village with a fine church and tithe-barn. It is well known for its well dressing tradition.

Turn right along the village street, bearing right at the T-junction, and then going left to the A6020. Follow the A6020 for a little over 325yds/m then go through a stile on the opposite side of the road, crossing a small stream before rising across a rough grass hillside to reach open fields. Head diagonally left across the next two fields. Enter the parkland of Churchdale Hall and skirt round the left-hand side of the field to reach a gate. Follow the field boundary a little further to another gate and go left, along a lane which soon joins the driveway from the hall. Pass Churchdale Farm to reach the A6020.

Turn right. After 325yds/m, just opposite Rowdale House Farm, a signposted, broad green track crosses the field to Cracknowl Wood. The steadily rising path passes through the wood, then heads across a field towards the left-hand side of the clump of trees where Cracknowl House comes into view. Head for the kissing gate and follow the path which now runs almost parallel to the wall. Look out for a stile near a big ash tree. An indistinct path bears right, crossing the brow of the hill before descending to the green lane over Holme Hall Pasture. Follow the lane down to the right, passing a dew pond.

The remains of Holme Hall Quarry are on the right, the highest workings of the Holme Bank Chert Mine. Chert is a very hard material used in potters' glaze. In the 18th and 19th centuries many of the big names of the Potteries were associated with the chert mines of Bakewell.

Continue down the track, with a fine view of Bakewell, soon reaching a gateway into a wood and descending more steeply.

On the left are more workings from the chert mine, still in use by a firm called Smiths Runners. Chert blocks were known as runners. At the bottom of the hill, the main entrance to the mine lies to the left.

At Holme Lane, go left, soon bearing right into Scott's Meadows. A delightful riverside walk back to the Bakewell Bridge completes the circuit.

22/7/05   13.3 m on ped.
THE COCK & PULLET AT SHELDON
— Worth going back to eat
V. good walk, good views, not
too strenuous
Saw hare, water vole, buzzard

21 Brassington and Aldwark

Gentle strolling in unusual limestone scenery, visiting two spectacular rock outcrops at Rainster and Harbro' as well as little-visited Aldwark. The walk includes a grand stretch of the Chariotway and some fine long distance views.

Distance: 7½ miles/12km	**Type of walk:** Easy strolling, mainly on little-used field paths, with some optional scrambling.
Height gain: 1,460ft/450m	
Walking time: 4 hours 30 minutes	
Start/Finish: Brassington Church. Limited roadside parking in village.	**Public transport:** Sparse Mon-Sat bus service from Matlock, Ashbourne and Wirksworth.

Go through the churchyard, going left at Back Lane. In 165yds/m, there is a stile on the right. Bear left up the hillside, through a stile, then bearing right. Cross the fields, hummocky with lead mine shafts and spoil, soon joining a narrow green lane and turning left. Opposite a ruined barn, there is a signposted stile on the right into a pathless field. Keep left of the low limestone crags, heading through scrub towards Rainster Rocks. Before the main group of rocks are two other tors. Pass between them, crossing another track and a stile, heading for the waymark post, then straight to the rocks.

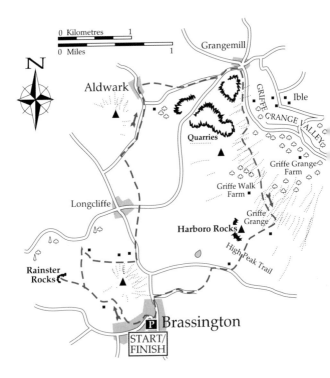

Rainster Rocks and its surroundings have been inhabited for thousands of years. The rocks are well defended by short tough trees, growing out of the cracks in the lime-stone. These and the general slipperiness of the rocks themselves make for an interesting ascent and descent.

Admire the views and return to the waymark post, turning left and going up the field to a gateway. Continue up the track, soon passing a barn and going through another gateway. Immediately beyond this, go through the second gate on the right, skirting round the barn to a short green lane. Turn left and pass through a gateway.

Follow a scanty path up mid-field, passing through a series of gateways, until almost on the brow of the hill, where the exit gateway is in the left-hand corner. Thereafter, bear right, following the left-hand wall to another gateway. Here bear left, still close to the wall, to reach the road.

Turn left for about 325yds/m, passing Longcliffe Dale Farm. Just before the electricity sub-station, there is an unsigned stile on the right. Bear left to reach a stile to the right of the sub-station. Skirt past the sub-station to a series of stiles round the back of Peak Quarry Farm onto a track, which bears right and left to the High Peak Trail.

It is hard to imagine that this was once a railway, closing as late as the 1960s. To the left was Longcliffe station, which for most of its long life only had a goods service. The severity of the curve into the station can clearly be seen. A stone sleeper from the 1830s' railway is built into the next stile.

Go over the Trail and down the step stile opposite, signposted to Aldwark. Head to the right of Long-cliffe works, towards the new building. Cross a rough track and pass to the left of the shed to reach the road. Turn right here for 100yds/m, then go left at a stile, into fields. Bear right, but just before the far corner go over a stile in the wall on the right. Go left, keeping beside the wall, passing through a series of fields to the road. Turn right here, following the road into Aldwark.

Harbro' Rocks lie to the right, whilst ahead the view is down Longcliffe Dale into the ever extending Grange Mill Quarries.

Keep straight on at a junction, then, just after the new house on the right, go right at a signpost, passing into open fields. Follow the left-hand wall down for about 100yds/m, then bear right, heading for the line of trees. Follow these for about 50 paces then bear right again, to a gateway. Bear diagonally left to the field corner and the road. Turn left, soon joining the B5056. Turn left, reaching Grange Mill in about 325yds/m.

This has always been an important junction of roads. The ancient north to south route, the Portway, came this way. Salt routes came over Bonsall Moor, passing through Grangemill before heading off through Aldwark to the west.

Turn right at the cross roads, then right again, heading up a track to a gate. This is the Portway. Follow the track up the hillside, soon rising far above the valley of the Via Gellia. At the next gate, bear left, contouring the hillside to a hidden gateway. Bear right, keeping company with the wall, soon reaching a signpost in the corner of the field. The Portway or Chariotway bears left along the obvious track, signposted to the High Peak Trail. The village on the far side of the Via Gellia is Ible.

Continue along the Chariotway for a mile/1.6km,

passing the access to Griffe Walk Farm and then reaching a fork in the track. Harbro' works can be seen on the skyline ahead, with new Harbro' Farm to the right. Turn sharp right, across the cattle grid and go along a grassy path, heading for the farm. Skirt to the right of the farm, on to the steep, open hillside. Keep straight on, uphill, to the right of the solitary tree, where a ruined stile takes the path into a very narrow field. The path is signed from here, but many people bear right to the trig point, which is now close.

There is a tremendous view from the summit, south to the distant line of Charnwood Forest, Cannock Chase and the Trent valley power stations; north through the nick between Wardlow Hay Cop and Longstone Edge, to Mam Tor.

Go south-east briefly, where a thorn bush marks a path down to the right. A short, flat open area follows, then a deepening gully cuts through the main rock band to pick up a good path. This descends past remains of old workings and ruined buildings before crossing the High Peak Trail and cutting through the edge of Hoben Works. Go down to the road and turn right.

After about 220yds/m go left, following the wall, with clay pits on the left and lead mines to the right The path soon descends steeply to join a road, which to the left ends abruptly in the clay pits. Turn right. Follow this pleasant lane down past limestone outcrops to the T-junction, turning left there to reach Brassington.

22 Castleton and Peak Forest

A stiff pull out of Castleton leads over the limestone moorland to Peak Forest. A dry dale and another climb leads to Sparrowpit. Here the walk leaves the limestone for the shales and grits of Rushup. The route over Rushup Edge is very popular, with wide views. The walk ends with a descent to Castleton via the impressive Mam Tor slip.

Distance:	No. 24 White Peak.
9¾ miles/16km.	**Type of walk:**
Height gain:	Mainly field paths and
1,820ft/560m.	tracks, with some steep
Walking time:	climbs at the start.
5-6 hours	**Public transport:**
Start/Finish:	Daily buses to
Castleton Bus Station.	Castleton from
GR152830.	Sheffield and Bakewell.
Pay/display car park at	Many additional
western end of village,	seasonal services.
GR149829.	Daily train service
Maps:	from Manchester and
OS Outdoor Leisure	Sheffield to Hope or
No. 1 Dark Peak and	Edale stations.

Castleton is an early example of a planned town. The Normans planted a market town here, protected by the castle and surrounded by the town ditch, parts of which still remain.

Go up Castle Street into the Square, turning right

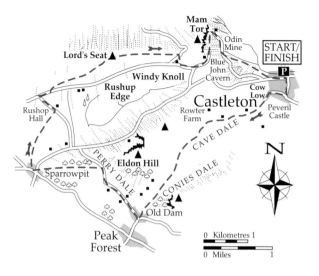

just beyond the youth hostel, following the signs to Peak Cavern. Cross Peakshole Water, and go up Goosehill to the point where the lane forks. Bear right, continuing up the hill. Soon the lane degenerates to a track and reaches a gate. At the end of the line of trees, ascend diagonally to the left.

Part way up the hillside, turn left along a track, which zigzags upwards, swinging to the right near the edge of Cave Dale. Continue along the flanks of Cow Low, with a widening view to the right, over the Lose Hill ridge to Kinder Scout. At a gate by a solitary tree, the route forks. Go right, signposted to Rowter Farm, rising over Hurdlow to reach a ladder stile. Go left by the wall.

The hummocks and hollows in the next field betray the presence of the "old man", an expression given to the exploits of the early lead miners by their 18th/19th-century successors.

Continue ahead, eventually passing to the right of a corrugated metal shed. Rowter Farm is to the right, with Mam Tor and Rushup Edge beyond. Continue upwards alongside the wall to a track.

This track was part of the prehistoric route linking settlements on the limestone plateau with the hill fort on Mam Tor. It continued in use throughout the Roman and Saxon period when it became known as the Portway.

Go left, through a gate, then bear right, across a rough field to a stile. Various narrow paths run through a riot of old workings to reach a track, close to a gate. Portway Mine can be seen to the left. Go through the gate and bear left, leaving the track. An obvious path heads away south-west, passing the gaping mouth of a lead mine shaft, inadequately capped.

Pass through a belt of trees, marking a line of old workings. Conies Dale can soon be seen to the left. Descend towards Peak Forest, soon bearing left at a fork. Head through a gap in the wall after which the path is more obvious. Pass through a series of stiles, soon reaching a narrow green lane, which shortly reaches Old Dam.

A short distance ahead lies the village of Peak Forest, with a church dedicated to Charles, King and Martyr, a most unusual dedication. This church also boasted the ability to marry elopers, with a minimum of residential qualification.

Turn right along Perry Dale, a classic dry limestone valley. After a little over 1,000yds/m, Rake Vein Plantation is reached, stretching up the hillside on the left.

Like many of these strips of trees, this one lies on the course of an old lead vein. When the mines were abandoned, the shafts and spoil were left for nature to restore the damage. Farmers helped by walling off the despoiled ground because of the risk to stock.

Go through the stile on the left, heading steeply uphill, alongside the plantation. Just before the end of the second field, a gate in the wall on the right leads into a narrow lane. Go almost to the far side of the wood, then bear left, through a gap. A distinct path twists its way through the wood, soon crossing back to the southern side.

Follow the path to a stile on the left leading back into fields. Bear right, heading diagonally towards the T-shaped pylon, and a stile, leading into a short lane. At the end of the lane bear left, heading towards Sparrowpit, roughly following the line of pylons. Negotiate a couple of step stiles before reaching the road. Here turn left, passing the Memorial Hall, before turning right into a farmyard, following a signpost to Rushup and Castleton.

From a hidden gate on the right, at the end of the buildings, an obvious path leads across fields towards Rushup Farm, soon reaching a stile. The path battles its way alongside a fence into the garden of the farmhouse.

Pass through the garden to the farm access. Bear left along a track by a barn, at the end of which, follow the waymarked route left, up the hill to a track, which soon swings to the left round the hillside. Bear right here and descend a rough bank to a waymarked stile. In the next field a path skirts to the left of boggy ground.

Head for a stile in the corner of the field, then continue through a series of fields, until a waymarked stile is reached. Bear left, up the hill, heading for the end of the tree belt and soon reaching a gate and the road, close to Rushup Hall. Go left, up Rushup Lane to the main road. Go right, and in 170yds/m bear left, up on to Rushup Edge. The broad, rough track climbs steadily, in a deep hollow-way. After 800yds/m, just past a gate, the route forks. Keep right here and continue along the ridge top.

The view is now very extensive, with the Vale of Edale, backed by Kinder Scout, to the left and the limestone plateau, marred by Eldon Hill Quarry, to the right. Mam Tor is straight ahead.

The walk along the summit ridge of Rushup and Lord's Seat is a delight. The summit is a small grassy mound to the left of the path. The ridge narrows, but all too soon a good track veers off to the right. Follow this down to the road and go left.

A short distance up the road, there is the choice of ascending Mam Tor or turning right following the signposted route to Blue John Cavern. (If an ascent of Mam Tor is added, return to the road at this point.) Drop steeply to reach the A625 again, close to the junction. Go left, on the old road past Blue John Cavern. The road swings across the face of Mam Tor, then ends, abruptly.

The scene of devastation is quite shocking and is a salutary reminder of the power of natural forces. The road was built from Castleton to Blue John in the early part of the 19th-century, to replace the steep Winnats Pass. The builders reckoned without the Shivering Mountain, for regularly the face of Mam Tor would slip and destroy their road. This collapse/rebuild cycle continued until 1976 when the road fell 3ft/1m overnight. Further major slips occurred and the road has never re-opened.

Walk down the collapsed road, round the hairpin bend to Odin Gorge, a spectacular cleft in the hillside, marking the junction of the limestone and shales.

On the left of the road is the former Odin lead mine, the workings of which extended westwards beneath the shale almost to Mam Nick. Today the site is still marked by the remains of a crushing circle and the capped shaft. The shaft is oval, which is very unusual.

Go down to the mine site and pass to the left of the crusher before dropping to a bridge. Skirt round to the right of Knowlegates Farm and through a series of stiles running alongside Odin Sitch, which was the drainage level for the mine.

The name "sitch" is pure Norse and crops up frequently in north-east Derbyshire and Yorkshire. Sometimes it appears as "sitch". Other times as "syke", or "sick".

Eventually, just over 800yds/m from the mine, the path goes right, soon passing through a narrow ginnel between houses, to the main road at Castleton. Turn left to reach the bus station and car park.

23 Elton and Gratton Dale

A gentle stroll across fields leads to Gratton. The delightful limestone valley of Gratton Dale follows, with a brief hiatus at the A5012 before joining a fine green lane with wide views. This leads eventually to Greenlow Farm. Little-used field paths take the walk across the Via Gellia and Winster Moor. Another fine green track, Islington Lane, leads down to the Elton Cross and back to Elton village.

Distance:	**Type of walk:**
8 miles/13km	Little-used field and
Height gain:	dale paths, green lanes
954ft/295m	and packhorse routes
Walking time:	with no steep
4 hours 30 minutes	climbing.
Start/Finish:	**Public transport:**
Elton (Duke of York)	Monday to Saturday
GR222609. Limited	buses to Elton from
roadside parking in	Matlock and Bakewell.
village.	

Go down Well Street by the church. After about 110yds/m, bear left where the road forks, to reach a signposted stile. Go left, following the wall to another signpost and passing through the gap in the hedge into the next field.

The views are quite extensive, with Stanton Moor to the right and Harthill Moor ahead. This field houses the Elton ski tow, so beware of skiers in winter.

Bear right and go down to the left-hand corner, continuing through the next field to the road. Go right briefly, then left at the signposted stile, following the left-hand wall through a couple of fields before bearing right just beyond a ruined barn. Pass through two more fields, then bear left to reach a signposted stile. Follow the wall on the right until a double stile is reached, then go straight ahead into an area of rough land. The path turns right here, following the hedge and wall, through the bushes to a well-hidden stile. It then bears right, dropping down through the rough grass and quagmire to a stile and the road at Gratton.

Turn left until the telephone box is reached, where signs point into Gratton Dale. Follow the obvious track, soon arriving at a well-preserved lime kiln. Pass through a gate, into the mouth of Gratton Dale, a fine example of a dry valley, though here and there evidence exists that water is not far below the surface. The path passes a pump house, now almost derelict, and soon reaches a clump of pines.

Beyond the pines the going becomes rough, with huge limestone boulders scattered about. The path twists and turns through the rocks until Mouldridge Grange comes into view, and the dale forks. To the right lies Long Dale, but go left here, making for Mouldridge Grange. About 110yds/m up from the bridlegate, bear left, climbing to a gateway on the lip of the dale. Carry straight on until a wall is reached. Follow this wall to the left and then right, to the A5012. Turn right here. There is a good view away to the right to the higher hills beyond Youlgreave. Longstone Edge can be seen in the distance.

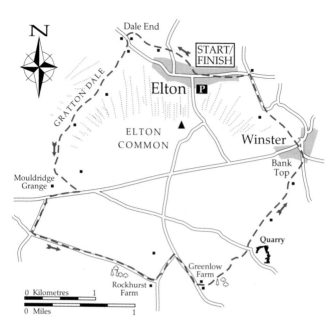

Follow the road down to the entrance to Mould-ridge Grange and there turn left, following the lane signed to Parwich for about 540yds/m, to reach a five-way junction.

To the right lies Pikehall. The belt of trees leading up the hillside from the hamlet marks the course of the Derby to Buxton Roman road. This remained in use until the late 18th century. The course of the Roman road from Pikehall to the five-way junction is marked by a double line of walls. Its exit was through the gate on the left, heading straight up the shoulder of the hill towards Minninglow. This is no longer a public right of way. To the left is a fine green lane, the continuation of the walk and the course of the early 18th-century Derby to Manchester road.

Go left here, along this wide green lane, keeping just below the ridge of Minninglow and Longedge, with an extensive view to the left, reaching to Longstone Edge and the East Moors. Apart from the occasional glimpse of traffic on the A5012, there is a splendid feeling of isolation on this track. It is not until Rockhurst Farm is reached, after 1¼ miles/2km, that any building is encountered.

Turn left at Rockhurst Farm, where the road to Longcliffe is joined. After 500yds/m, turn right at the T-junction, rising steadily to reach the brow of the hill, just before Greenlow Farm.

Go down the drive to Greenlow Farm, passing the farmhouse on the right. Just past the barn on the left, go left to reach a double set of gates on the right, leading into fields. Head for the left-hand end of the plantation, the stile being marked by a solitary thorn. Bear left, passing over the brow of the hill, soon reaching the remains of a wall. Head for the large thorn at the left-hand end of the wall and then go straight ahead, diagonally left across the field, making for the obvious gateway. Ivon-brook Quarry is in view ahead.

Pass through the gateway and follow the wall up to the left, topping the rise and beginning the descent into the Via Gellia, soon encountering a squeeze stile. Bear right across a pathless field on steep ground, soon reaching the road by the wood.

Go through the signposted stile opposite, following the wall until it strikes away to the left. A narrow path continues uphill, heading for an obvious gateway. To the right is the screen mound for Ivonbrook Quarry. As the path nears the gateway, it veers to the right to another, less obvious gate in the field corner. Make for the two pylons close together. As the path climbs, a gateway comes into view, leading into Sacheveral Lane. (There is a quick way back to Elton from here. Simply turn left and follow the lane for about $1^1/4$ miles/2km.)

To the right, quarry workings have severed Sacheveral Lane. Cross the lane, bearing left up the field to a stile in the far corner. Continue on the same alignment to a stile by a thorn bush. Bear right in this next field, which is pathless. On crossing the brow of the hill there are numerous gaps in the wall ahead, but the stile lies almost in the far corner. Go through the stile, then left beside the wall to another stile.

Follow the fence on the right to a stile, just before the tall trees. Bear left, avoiding the covered reservoir and head towards the prominent clump of trees. Keep heading for these trees through a series of fields and across a green lane, finally reaching the road.

At the road go left, passing Winster Mere, then going left along the lane signed to Elton and Newhaven. At the cross roads go straight on, along a walled track. (Just to the right lies the Miners Standard inn, the only source of refreshment on the entire walk.) Carry on along Islington Lane, part of the ancient Portway, or Derbygate. Keep right where the lane forks and soon begin to descend quite sharply, in a fine hollow-way. On the right is the limestone knoll known as Grey Tor.

The turnpike road can be seen below and there is a good view across to Stanton Moor. Carry on along Islington Lane, which dips to a cross roads, rises briefly and soon reaches Elton Cross. Here the Elton to Winster road cuts across the old road. Turn left, passing the continuation of the Portway on the right and follow the road back into Elton.

24 Kniveton and Tissington Ford

A stroll over Wigber Low leads to the famous Tissington Ford. The walk next visits Parwich, with grand views into the heart of the limestone Peak. The route then passes Ballidon church and the end of Hipley Dale before climbing to Bradbourne. Then it is down into Havenhill Dale from where a fine green lane climbs back to Kniveton.

Distance:	*Type of walk:*
7¼ miles/12km	*Easy walking,*
Height gain:	*generally on little-used*
925ft/285m	*field paths and tracks,*
Walking time:	*with one ascent of note*
4 hours	*Public transport:*
Start/Finish: Kniveton	*Kniveton has a sparse*
School. GR211502.	*Monday to Saturday*
Limited roadside	*bus service from*
parking in village.	*Ashbourne and*
	Matlock.

Walk along Longrose Lane, following the caravan site sign. After 435yds/m, bear right, following signs to New House Farm. In 300yds/m, go left down a rough track, towards a red-brick farmhouse. Go left here, with a fine view down Wigber Dale. Pass the farmhouse, skirting to the left of the stables, onto a green lane. Follow this into open fields. Follow the left-hand hedge then go right, along a line of trees, to the top of the hill. Go through a gate, following

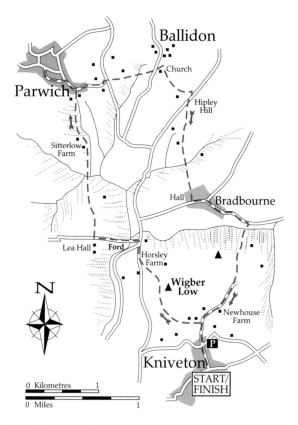

the left-hand wall, with the summit of Wigber Low to the right. Continue over the flank of Wigber Low, down into the valley of Bradbourne Brook.

Bradbourne village lies to the right. Ahead there is a good view towards Tissington, the White Peak and the higher gritstone moors beyond.

About 500yds/m from Wigber Low, a farm track joins. The descent continues, at times steeply, to the road near Tissington Ford. At the ford, use the pedestrian bridge and follow the lane up the hill, passing over a cattle grid and turning right at a footpath sign, pointing to Parwich. Follow the broad green track, almost to the corner of the field. Ignore the first gate and stile on the right, carrying on to reach a waymarked gate, there turning left.

Follow the wall for about 165yds/m, then bear right, descending to a double stile. Climb to a gateway, then skirt round the hillside, with Gorsehill Farm below. The path bears left, making for the clump of pines. Pass over a dubious stile, making for the right of the electricity pylon and then the large willow before crossing a bridge. Follow the fence almost to the end of the field, before bearing right to a gateway then right again, to another gateway. Keep to the right-hand edge of the field. Pass through Sitterlow farmyard, before reaching open fields again. Then continue straight on through two fields to a green lane.

Pass Parwich sewage works on the left after 435yds/m. Swing to the right, passing a pumping station on the left, then go left through a stile. Continue by a stream, passing through a number of fields, to the memorial bridge. Continue to the road and turn right. (Parwich village lies just to the left.) Follow the road for 800yds/m to a T-junction. Go straight ahead, through a gate into fields. Keep to the left-hand side to a bridge, marked with a white plastic arrow. Cross the bridge and head to a waymarked stile. Bear left in the next field, making for a stile to the right of the clump of pines. Go up the left of the field to the road and turn left. Turn right at the signpost to Ballidon church.

The church stands in splendid isolation in the middle of a field, surrounded by a wall. It is a simple building, no tower or spire, just a nave and a single bell.

Pass to the right of the church on to a rough track and turn right, skirting the flank of the hill. Where the track forks, keep left, passing through a gate and stile. Where the track swings right, carry on alongside the hedge, descending to the road, with Hipley Dale to the left. Go right, then left at a footpath sign, bearing right to a stone stile. Follow the left-hand hedge, ignoring the gateway. Pass through a gateway in the hedge ahead, making for the solitary tree, then to the left of Dulands Farm.

Follow the obvious path and cross Mellowmeadow Brook. Bradbourne church tower is in view through the trees ahead. Climb alongside the hedge to a stile in the top left-hand corner, marking the boundary of the parkland surrounding Bradbourne church and hall. Keep straight on, passing between hall and church.

Go through the churchyard, admiring the Norman tower and ancient cross. Then go down the drive to the road. Go left, passing the front gate of the Hall. Bear right at the junction, following the signs to Carsington and Kniveton. The road soon dips into Havenhill Dale and an unsigned track leads off to the right. Cross Havenhilldale Brook, beyond which the track rises sharply.

Pass through a series of gates, soon reaching the top of the hill. A level stretch follows, until a narrow lane is joined, just by a reservoir on the right. Bear right, soon descending past New House Farm and crossing the head of Wigber Dale. Just beyond the farm a track goes off right, marking the point where the outward route is rejoined. Go straight on, retracing the outward route to Kniveton.

25 Middleton Dale and Friden

A quick exit from Middleton leads into Middleton Dale. A steady climb follows, before reaching Long Dale. The Roman road is joined briefly at Friden-mouth, then the High Peak Trail to Brundcliffe. A classic green lane passes Mere Farm, before the final stroll past Rake Wood to Middleton by Youlgreave.

Distance: 7½ miles/12km.	parking at Friden picnic site, GR172607.
Height gain: 860ft/265m	**Type of walk:** Easy dale and trail walking, with no serious ascents.
Walking time: 4-4½ hours	
Start/Finish: Middleton Square. GR195632. Limited roadside parking in village. Alternative	**Public transport:** Middleton has a Monday to Saturday bus service to Bakewell.

Follow the lane signed to Elton, turning left in less than 50yds/m down a farm track. Pass Green Farm, descending a classic limestone dale, with substantial crags on either side, soon reaching Middleton Dale. Turn right along a good path, which soon passes over a spring surging out of the rocks on the right. Crags hem in the path closely, until it is forced to cross the river. Soon the path goes up a flight of steps to avoid another small crag. Go right, briefly, but then descend right, to another bridge.

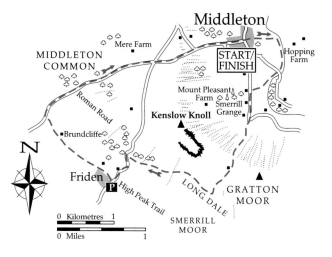

In this short space the scenery has changed dramatically, from confined limestone dale to wide shale valley.

Across the stream, bear right, up the slope to locate the first of a series of stiles through the fields. Soon a little enclosure is reached with a barn on the left. Beyond this, follow the left-hand wall to a narrow lane. Go through a stile opposite, keeping close to the stream. The valley becomes more dale-like again as the path passes back on to limestone. Locate a stile on the left, turning right, keeping close to the fence. Ascend quite steeply, with the thickly wooded limestone dale below you, keeping close to the edge to find the route down, which starts by a large ash. A stile soon leads on to Elton Lane. Turn left for about 550yds/m. Where the road turns left, go up a narrow, walled track, soon reaching open fields. Slant up to the left to join another track, continuing up the dale. After about 550yds/m, go through a gate into a lane, which bends to the right and widens by three gates. Go through the middle gate, keeping left and passing a dew pond.

The view ahead becomes more extensive as the climb proceeds, with Alec Low prominent. The sudden appearance of Long Dale, which opens up ahead, is quite a surprise.

Pass through a gate on to the dale edge and turn right, following the wall to a water tank. Bear left, through the clumps of gorse, soon descending through limestone boulders, heading towards Bolderstone Plantation. There swing left, dropping into the dale bottom to join a path coming up the valley. Keep right here, following the plantation wall. Carry on along the main dale, with the larches of Little Bolderstone Plantation to the left. A gateway on the left accesses a narrow-walled lane which follows the plantation wall to the left.

Here the bridleway joins the former Roman road, which came through the cutting to the left. This remained in use until the A515 was built in the early 19th century. This area was referred to by an 18th-century traveller as "Stoney Fridenmouth". In those days this junction was a crossroads and the bridleway ascended the rocky field to Friden.

Turn right along a terrace on the south side of Long Dale, until the way is barred by a dry-stone embankment. Just before the embankment, turn left up a track which soon meets the road. Carry on along the road, pass under the bridge, which once carried the Cromford and High Peak Railway, turn left up the access to Friden "station" and left again at the High Peak Trail.

It is hard to imagine that the trail was once a railway and that it formed a vital part of the local economy, serving agriculture, quarries, brickworks like Friden and even providing a sparse passenger service at one time.

Continue along the trail for about 1¼ miles/1.75km, passing the brickworks, the 18-milestone and Bruncliffe Farm, before reaching a "level crossing", where Green Lane crosses the "line". Turn right here. Green Lane crosses the head of Long Dale before reaching the trees that mark the Roman road line.

The hummocks and hollows indicate workings for silica sand, a vital ingredient for the firebricks produced at Friden. It was the presence of this raw material that led to the establishment of the factory in the first place. The pits were originally served by an extensive narrow gauge railway system.

Continue over the brow of Middleton Common, before descending past Mere Farm to a cross roads. Go down the lane signposted to Middleton, descending steadily, passing Rake Wood on the right. On the left, in a small field near the turreted house, is a small area of limestone "pavement", quite a rarity in the Peak.

Pass one of the village wells on the left and so reach the centre of Middleton.

26 Millers Dale and Wormhill

A stroll along the Monsal Trail leads into Chee Dale and up to Wormhill. The walk continues across fields into Peter Dale and then through Monks Dale back to Millers Dale.

Distance:
6 miles/10km
Height gain:
780ft/523m
Walking time:
3 hours 30 minutes
Start/Finish:
Millers Dale Old Station. GR138732. Pay/display parking at the old station.

Type of walk:
Dale walking at its best, but in parts jungle-like and very rough underfoot.
Public transport:
Millers Dale has daily buses from Buxton, Tideswell and Sheffield.

From the old station, proceed west along the Monsal Trail. Until 1967 there was a main line railway here, with a five platform station and a goods yard. On the right are the remains of the cattle dock, then Millers Dale quarry sidings. A little further on is a fine example of a water tank, fed by a hydraulic ram from the River Wye, far below. Finally, on the right again are the huge restored lime kilns for Millers Dale quarry.

Just beyond the lime kilns the trackbed narrows on the approach to a fine brick/stone viaduct. Bear

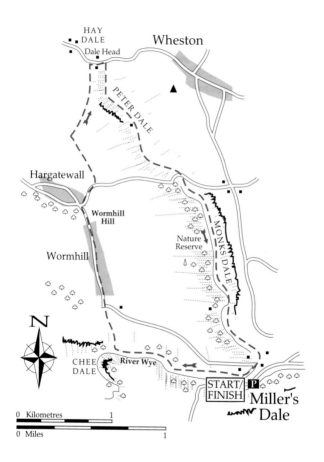

HAY
DALE
Wheston
Dale Head

PETER DALE

Hargatewall

Wormhill
Hill

MONKS DALE

Nature
Reserve

Wormhill

N

CHEE
DALE
River Wye

START/
FINISH
Miller's
Dale

P

0 Kilometres 1

0 Miles 1

right just before the viaduct, descending steep slopes to the river. Turn right, following the Wye upstream, a lovely walk.

Soon the path is joined by another route near a footbridge. Here go right, ascending from the dale, making use of a natural incline of limestone slabs. The slabs lead unerringly through scrub and gorse, past patches of limestone grassland containing a myriad of flowers.

After the path levels out at a viewpoint, the route forks. Go right, turning into Wormhill Dale, a narrow side valley. Proceed through woodland, eventually passing into a narrow, walled track leading to the road at Chee Tor Cottage. Bear left and go through the village of Wormhill. Pass Wormhill Hall on the right. Where a lane goes off right, to the church, leave the road, following the path parallel to the road, passing Brindley Memorial.

This commemorates the great 18th-century canal pioneer James Brindley, who transformed the transport system of the country. A short distance beyond the memorial are the village stocks.

Carry straight on, passing the old school on the right and the solitary standing stone in the adjacent field. Continue up the road, passing a lane on the right, where there is a sudden and surprising view to the east, taking in Tideslow and Sir William Hill, both easily distinguished by their television masts. About 200yds/m further on the road splits three ways. Take the right-hand route, with Hargate Hall to the left.

Descend steadily, swinging to the north, but where the lane turns sharply right, go left, over a stile. Follow the left-hand wall, down through a series of fields, then turn left through a gateway, just before a ruined barn. Skirt round the barn, thus locating a stile in the wall corner. Continue through a couple more fields until a rather larger field is reached. Bear right here, making for the left of the tree belt.

In the next field, bear left, to a track, following it to a gate and stile. Peter Dale can be seen ahead, but there is no way into it from here. Follow the wall almost to the end of the field, then bear left to a stile in the end wall, on the dale edge. Skirt to the left, round the dale edge, soon picking up a wall on the right and entering a narrow-walled track. This leads down to and round Dale Head Farm, and on to the road. Go right, turning right again in about 100yds/m, into Peter Dale.

This is normally a dry limestone valley, but in wet weather there can be a stream large enough to make the passage of this dale very difficult. If this is the case, do not venture into Monks Dale. Instead, follow the waymarked Limestone Way back to Millers Dale.

Low limestone crags soon begin to crowd the path. In spring the meadowland between these crags is covered with flowers, a beautiful sight. The next section of the dale is very narrow, but it soon broadens out again and swings left, only to narrow once more. This section is very rough underfoot.

Again the dale widens abruptly and the path joins

the road left earlier at Hargatewall. (The Limestone Way turns left here, following the road.) Now enter Monks Dale, which is a National Nature Reserve, so please be very careful. Normally this is a dry dale, except near Millers Dale. In some places the path is the river bed. The dale narrows sharply with dramatic rock scenery. A stile leads into the heavily wooded section of the valley. Twist and turn through the trees, often very rough underfoot, sometimes in the riverbed itself, sometimes on open scree. This interesting exercise goes on for about a 1,000yds/m.

The path then reaches a stile and abruptly bears off left, up the hillside to emerge on open grassland above a line of low crags. A selection of paths presents itself, but all go in the same direction, following the course of the stream, which here runs more frequently, though never all year round.

The paths converge to pass along the top of a line of crags, quite high above the stream. As the path turns a corner, the dramatic limestone cliffs on the south side of Millers Dale come into view. Descend to stream level again, soon reaching a bridge, beyond which the path rises away up the western side of the dale, developing into a track with a wall to the left. An abrupt right turn takes the path up to a kissing gate and Glebe Farm.

There is a grand view of the two spectacular Millers Dale viaducts. The nearer one is the newer of the two, being built about 1900. The southern one is built in wrought iron and was constructed in the early 1860s. The Monsal Trail goes over the old viaduct.

Go past Glebe Farm, over a stile onto the road and turn left. The station car park lies just to the right. Public transport users should carry on, under the bridges, down to the main road and the bus stop.

27 Taddington, Pomeroy and Flagg

A sharp pull out of Taddington leads to Sough Top then across the plateau to Pomeroy. Negotiating the maze of fields is the principal difficulty in the rest of the walk, which passes through the straggling village of Flagg and over Taddington Moor before returning to Taddington.

Distance:
7 miles/11km
Height gain:
988ft/304m
Walking time:
4 hours
Start/Finish:
Taddington (Queens Arms). GR142711. Limited roadside parking in village.
Type of walk:
Green lanes and field paths over the plateau, some quite tricky to follow, but only one main ascent.
Public transport:
Taddington has daily buses from Manchester, Stockport, Buxton, Leek, the Potteries, Bakewell, Matlock, Sheffield, Derby and Nottingham.

Walk up the main street, passing the church of St. Michael and All Angels, soon reaching a road junction. Turn left up Humphrey Gate then right, through a stile, up a narrow path beside Harrison's Garage, soon reaching steep fields. Bear right up the field, then left at the next stile, soon reaching a narrow road. Follow the sign to Chelmorton. Climb the shoulder of the hill, passing through a couple

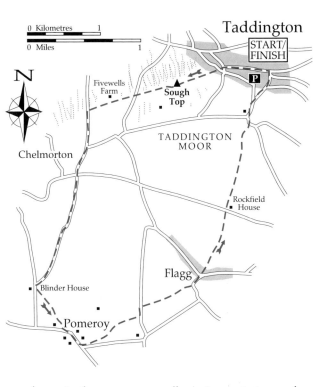

of gaps in the numerous walls. A signpost at one of these is a useful clarification of the route. As the path climbs there is an ever extending view to the right, over Millers Dale and up Monks Dale, to the higher hills of the Dark Peak.

Ahead is the "summit" of Sough Top, but, closer inspection reveals that it is a reservoir. Keep to the left of the reservoir. The true summit of Sough Top lies just to the right, beyond the reservoir, marked by a trig point. Continue across the nearly level grass, passing through a number of stiles, following the right-hand wall.

An increasingly good view opens up towards Buxton and the Axe Edge moors. There is some evidence of former lead mining on this stretch, with the occasional capped shaft.

Cross a green lane, resuming the unerring course beside the wall thereafter, and in 400yds/m reach Five Wells Farm.

The farm's name derives from a series of springs, vital anywhere, but especially so on the limestone. However, the name is better known for the well-preserved chambered cairn, which lies north of the farm.

Beyond the farm the path reaches a rough, tarred lane. Go left, dropping gently to reach the road. Bear right, with surprisingly wide views on both sides. In about 400yds/m go straight ahead at a cross roads, along the rough green lane. Soon Blinder House is seen ahead, and slightly to the left, the houses of Pomeroy. The lane joins a road, but go left at a signposted stile, a short cut to Pomeroy. Follow the right-hand wall, through a couple of fields to an obvious dale head.

The field beyond this wall contained the Buxton to Derby Roman road, but it would take an expert to distinguish any signs now.

In the valley bottom go over a stile on the right, by an electricity pole, and head straight across to the prominent stile. Do not cross it, but turn left, alongside the wall. Gradually climbing, the path soon reaches the A515, with the Pomeroy village hall to the right. Weigh up which is safer; to cross the road on to the footway, only to have to recross in about 150yds/m, or to stay on the east side of the road at this notoriously dangerous bend.

Pomeroy consists of Street Farm, Pomeroy Cottages and the Duke of York pub. Both farm and cottages are built on the Roman road alignment. The place-name Street is a common indicator of a Roman route.

Just beyond the pub, go left at a signposted stile. Bear right in the field to reach a gateway. Here bear left to a stile in the middle of the wall.

Flagg can be seen ahead, a straggle of houses and farms. It has its moments, for on Easter Tuesday there are the Flagg Races, a point-to-point through these very fields, with the walls as the jumps.

Head to the far right-hand corner. This stile is followed within a few yards by a stile on the left. Bear right, passing the pond in mid-field, heading for the clump of trees. Skirt the remains of Pasture Barn to another gate, beyond which the footpath runs alongside the wall to reach a narrow lane. Turn left, but in 100yds/m go right, at a signpost. Follow the right-hand wall, proceeding through a series of fields, with lead mine spoil heaps to the left, to reach a road. Go left, passing the Nursery school. At the T-junction go straight ahead, up a track towards Flagg Hall Farm.

The farm is made up of some very fine old buildings, one

barn bearing the date 1681. The hall is of similar vintage.

Pass through the farmyard and continue along a track. Half way down the field, bear left to reach a stile by some new trees and a pond. Wriggle through the trees and then go straight on, heading for a clump of mature trees, reaching a road at the end of this long field. Go right, but turn left in 100yds/m, beside Rockfield House.

Follow the broad green lane, probably a lead mine access. The track kinks right and left at what looks suspiciously like a shaft top. About 150yds/m further on, go over a stile on the right, bearing left to a stile in the far wall, passing some very prominent spoil heaps.

Head for the gateway in the top right-hand corner, clip the corner of the next field, bearing slightly right to a broad green lane. Cross and head straight up the shallow valley to a stile in the middle of the northern wall. Bear right, around the knoll to the far right-hand corner of the field, heading diagonally across the next field to reach the road. Bear left at the T-junction, on the Taddington road, soon bearing right at a clump of trees, into a narrow green lane. Follow the steep lane to emerge in Taddington, just by a chapel. Turn left for the Queens Arms.

28 Bradford and Lathkill Dales

The walk begins in Youlgreave before descending into Bradford Dale. A climb up Lomberdale to Moor Lane and Long Rake follows. A gentle stroll over the limestone plateau soon leads to Cales Dale and thence into the National Nature Reserve of Lathkill Dale. A grand riverside stroll then follows, passing Over Haddon and Conksbury before ascending Coalpit Lane to Youlgreave.

Distance:
7¼ miles/12km
Height gain:
990feet/305m
Walking time:
4 hours
Start/Finish:
Youlgreave Church.
Limited roadside

parking in village.
Type of walk:
Fine dale walking on
well-defined paths.
Some steep ascents and
descents.
Public transport:
Youlgreave has daily
buses from Bakewell.

From Youlgreave church, go west along the main street, passing the pump, and the Co-op, now the youth hostel. About 150yds/m further on, turn left down Holywell, descending into Bradford Dale. Cross the river and turn right.

The River Bradford is a tamed stream, with many weirs for fishing. The water is beautifully clear and the birdlife numerous. With the clarity of the water, it is fascinating to watch the antics of the diving birds.

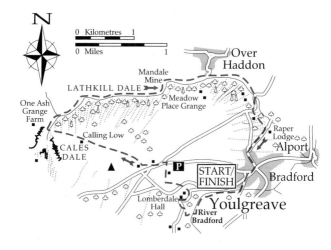

After 1,000yds/m turn right to cross a bridge. Zig-zag steeply uphill into Lomberdale, a side shoot of Bradford Dale. The path runs on top of low lime-stone crags, soon reaching the road. Go right, with Lomberdale Hall to the left. Where the road bends right again, go left at a stile, climbing up the field to reach another road.

Go left for 100yds/m then right, over a stile. Head up across the field, to a stile, left of a gate. Follow a line of tall trees, to a stile by an ash. Go right, soon entering the back of Moor Lane picnic site. Pass through the picnic site, going left at the road.

On the right, posts indicate part of the site of Long Rake Mine. On the left the lead rake continues as a deep, open cut. There are at least five lower levels, some of which are flooded. The mine runs west for about a mile/1.6km.

At the junction with Conksbury Lane, go over the waymarked stile opposite, bearing left across the field, heading towards the pylons. Bear right at the next stile and left at the next one. A couple more stiles lead into Low Moor Plantation. Pass through the trees to a stile. Skirt round the right-hand end of Calling Low Farm, through a couple of kissing gates into another plantation. Go through the wood, into fields again.

The character of the walk now changes. In place of the limestone plateau, the cliffs of Lathkill Dale are seen to the right. Ahead lies the deep cleft of Cales Dale. Monyash can be seen ahead, with One Ash Grange on the opposite side of Cales Dale.

Descend through fields to the edge of Cales Dale, which is a National Nature Reserve. The descent into Cales Dale is steep, slippery and uneven. At the dale bottom, cross the stile and bear right, soon passing a spring. On reaching Lathkill Dale, cross the river and turn right below the impressive cliffs, following the riverside path, soon reaching a waterfall.

At the waterfall, the river plunges over a shelf of tufa rock. More water emerges from beneath the tufa. In very dry summers this waterfall is dry and it has proved possible to penetrate the caves beneath the tufa. Such explorations are only for the expert, and should not be attempted.

The remains of a mill are soon reached. The track passes through dense woodland, along a low embankment, with the river on the right. The path enters an open area, across which march some ruined stone piers.

These piers carried the water course across the valley to Mandale Mine. Originally they would have carried a wooden aqueduct.

Pass between the piers, soon reaching the remains of Mandale Mine on the left.

Do not venture into any of the shafts or adits. The remains of the engine house and wheel pit can clearly be seen, and in winter, when the leaves have fallen, the flue and the steam engine chimney can be discerned.

Continue down dale, soon crossing Mandale Sough Tail. Continue along the track, leaving the wood and soon reaching Lathkill Lodge. Go right at the Lodge and then left, alongside the river.

Soon the path reaches the main Lathkill resurgence, climbing away from the river briefly before descending again and continuing along the valley bottom. Over Haddon lies to the left. At Conksbury Bridge, turn right and cross the river. Go round the right-hand bend, then turn left along an unsigned but obvious footpath. Pass through a series of fields until Raper Lane is reached. Turn right. A short sharp climb soon levels out as the first houses of Youlgreave are sighted and the lane passes White House Farm. Turn left at Conksbury Lane and follow the road into the centre of Youlgreave.

The Staffordshire Moorlands

The area covered by this section is the gritstone and shale territory of the Upper Hamps and Manifold valleys, and the headwaters of the Dane and Churnet. It is a wild, upland area with few substantial villages and many scattered farms, mainly given over to sheep and cattle. The A523 marks the effective southern and western boundary.

The main English watershed almost follows the course of the A53 road from Buxton to Leek. The Dove, Manifold, Hamps and Churnet all drain to the Trent and the east coast. The Dane drains west to the Mersey. The watershed is not a spectacular ridge, except at the Roaches, where the gritstone outcrops grandly for one last time before plunging to the Midland plain.

Many of the paths in the area are little walked, but there are places where path erosion is a serious issue. The Roaches are a case in point, but a book covering this area would be incomplete without a walk over this superb ridge. Other popular spots include Three Shires Head, where Derbyshire, Cheshire and Staffordshire meet, and Rudyard Lake, right on the fringe of the White Peak map but well worth a visit.

The few villages have their interesting features too. Flash claims to be the highest village in England. Former inhabitants made use of their proximity to the county boundaries to indulge in counterfeiting coin, escaping over the border when prosecution threatened. In Longnor, there is a fine market place and market hall. One of the pubs in the village is the Crew and Harpur Arms, a name which commemorates the main landowning family of the area, the Harpur-Crews. Much of the estate passed into the ownership of the Peak National Park in lieu of death duties.

Tracks and paths criss-cross the area, many of considerable antiquity. Some are obviously packhorse routes and there are a number of fine examples of packhorse bridges, of which those at Three Shires Head are probably the most famous. The main commodity was salt from Cheshire to the farms of the moorlands and further east to the more populated parts of Derbyshire and Yorkshire.

Large tracts of the moorlands are used by the army for training, sometimes using live ammunition. The walks avoid these areas, but a rambler is likely to encounter camouflaged, gun-wielding soldiers on some of the paths, whilst the Roaches and Ramshaw Rocks are likely to be festooned with climbers.

This is a hard landscape and life on these hillfarms is a struggle too. Do not make life any harder by your walking.

29 Flash Bar and Three Rivers

A walk into three counties and to three of the main rivers of the Peak District. The route uses some rarely-travelled paths near the headwaters of the Dove and Manifold, as well as visiting the popular Three Shires Head.

Distance:
8 miles/13km
Height gain:
1,380ft/455m
Walking time:
4-5 hours
Start/Finish:
Flash Bar. GR032678. Limited roadside parking. Alternative parking at Gradbach

car park, GR998662.
Type of walk:
Little-used and rough field paths and easy packhorse routes. Some tricky navigation.
Public transport:
Flash Bar has daily bus services from Leek, the Potteries, Buxton, Bakewell and Sheffield.

From Flash Bar, go down the Longnor road for about 100yds/m, then go left at the footpath sign. Skirt to the right of the barn, then down the field, keeping to the right of the shallow valley. At the stile in the bottom, turn right to the road and then go left. Where the lane bends to the right the little stream to the left is the Dove. Even here it is the boundary between Derbyshire and Staffordshire.

Just before the bridge go over a stile on the right. Climb to another stile on top of the bank, then fol-

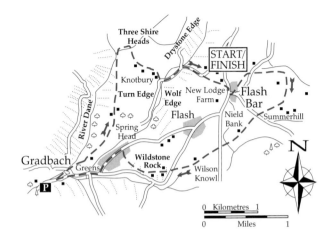

low the fence/wall, soon reaching Nether Colshaw Farm on the right. Just past the farm go right, by the pylon, follow the right-hand wall to a stile just beyond the farm. Turn left along the farm track, following this to the lane. Go right, soon reaching a T-junction by Summerhill Farm. Go straight across, into fields. Keep left of the barn to a stile, then bear right to the field corner.

To the left there is a tremendous view of the Upper Dove and Manifold valleys. The Roaches are also in view.

Packhorse grooves lead right, along the top of the Manifold slope, but the path slants left to Nield Bank Farm. Pass through the farmyard, then keep left at the fork. Cross the culverted Manifold and climb up to the A53. Go over the road into rough fields, bearing left to a footbridge over a ditch. Head to the right of Wilson Knowl Farm, negotiating another stream before reaching the farm track. Go straight across, right of the farm buildings, through a boggy wasteland of nettles and tussock grass, gradually bearing left to a steep descent to a meeting point of two small streams, guarded by a broken wall and barbed wire, with no stile.

Somehow cross the stream flowing down from the right, and head up the far slope. Stiles can then be seen ahead and a signpost marks the exit on to the road. At the road, go left, then right, along a track towards Wildstone Farm.

This track gives fine views to the west, to Bosley Minn, the Cheshire plain and the tele-communications tower on Sutton Common.

At the farm, keep right, turning left by the last barn. A gate leads into open fields and a faint track bears right, descending past a well to a gateway in the far wall. Head for a stile in the wall ahead, but turn sharp left before it is reached, to pass through a less obvious stile in the left-hand wall. Follow the right-hand wall down to a barn and signpost. Turn right along an obvious path, which soon curves to the north and reaches Spring Head Farm. At the lane by the farm go left, following the road past New Cottage to the T-junction and going right. Go along the road for about 500yds/m to the fork.

Those parking at Gradbach follow the signs to the Peter Watson camp site and YHA. Gradbach car park is about 350yds/m along this lane. If starting from the car park, follow the mill stream to the foot bridge and go left. A path alongside the river runs through a triangular field to a stile. Turn right, then left at the footpath sign.

Those not parked at Gradbach ignore the little lane forking off to the left, instead continuing ahead to a footpath sign and there go right.

All users then follow the signs and stiles into fields. Continue through a series of gateways and stiles, heading generally north-east. Just after a prominent ladder stile, bear left, making for the ruined cottage through a series of fields. Skirt to the left of the cottage and then right to a walled track.

Shuttlingslow can be seen to the left whilst the view back takes in the Roaches and Hen Cloud. The River Dane, seen away to the left, forms the boundary between Staffordshire and Cheshire. Turn left at the track and follow it for about a mile/1.6km to Three Shires Head.

Cheshire, Derbyshire and Staffordshire meet here and these footpaths and bridleways were once main roads. The large pool beneath the Derbyshire/Cheshire bridge is known as Panniers Pool, in recognition of its long use by packhorses.

The first bridge reached takes the path across from Staffordshire to Derbyshire. There is no need to go across the bridge to the left which links Derbyshire to Cheshire. Leave Three Shires Head by the Derbyshire track, soon climbing away from the Dane valley, following a tributary stream. After 300yds/m the track forks. Keep right, crossing the stream to enter a narrow, walled lane, which soon becomes a proper, tarred road.

The lane soon swings right, passing Knotbury Farm to a T-junction. Turn left and follow the narrow road, keeping right at the next two junctions. Climb past Oxensitch Farm before levelling out near New Lodge Farm, where suddenly Flash Bar and the hills of the limestone Peak come into view. Turn right at the main road to reach the bus stops, and the Travellers Rest.

30 Leek, Morridge and Ashenhurst

An interesting walk over some little-used paths leads to Morridge, a fine vantage point. The descent via Morridge Side and the traverse of Revedge to Ashenhurst opens up some fine views. The final stretch back to Leek involves an unusual flyover.

Distance:	**Type of walk:**
7 miles/11km	Little-used field paths
Height gain:	and a high moorland
1,170ft/360m	road. No difficult
Walking time:	ascents/descents.
4 hours	**Public transport:**
Start/Finish:	Leek has daily bus
Leek (Moorlands	services from the
Hospital) for public	Potteries, Manchester,
transport users.	Stockport,
Mount Road layby	Macclesfield, Sheffield,
near Pikehall Farm for	Bakewell, Buxton,
car bound walkers.	Ashbourne and Derby.

From the A523, go up the road on the north side of the Moorlands Hospital, to join Mount Road. Go right for about 100yds/m, then left along a footpath signed to Morridge. (Car users should walk north along Mount Road, passing Springfield old people's home, and then go right at the Morridge signpost). A narrow, walled path soon leads into fields, revealing a view to the left to Ramshaw Rocks, Hen Cloud, the Roaches and Shuttlingslow.

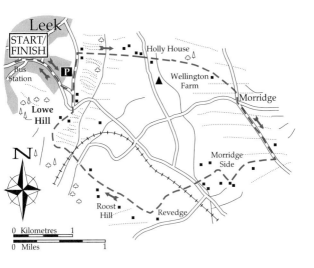

Descend steeply into a hidden valley, crossing the bridge in the bottom. Go left, then right, on to a track which immediately forks. Keep left of the fence, before turning right over a waymarked stile, bearing left up the field. Pass between big hawthorn bushes, keeping steeply sloping ground to the right. Continue up to the top of the field to a stile.

Do not follow the track to the right, but go straight ahead towards the farm, thus finding a stile. Follow the left-hand fence, passing to the left of the buildings. Turn left along the farm access, but immediately go right, up a short flight of steps. Go left, skirting to the right of the house, parallel with the lane on the left, heading towards Stile House Farm. Head left of the farm, through a couple of stiles, to reach the lane. Cross the lane, going over a waymarked stile.

Bear left to a stile, then bear right, swinging round the end of the buildings and cutting across the field to a bridge. Bear right again to a rough track. Here turn left, following the track until it forks. Go straight ahead, through a gateway and at once go right, over a stile, heading for a well-hidden stile by the large ash. Follow the hedge and fence left, up to a stile, left of the ruined Beeley Barn. Bear right in the rough field, skirting round the end of the fence, then heading uphill across a depression to a stile in the fence.

Clip the corner of the next field to a solitary gatepost, then strike across to the point where the stone wall descending from Morridge reaches the fence at the end of the field. Head across the slope, keeping to the left of the fence surrounding Well Farm, with a couple of leaning stones marking the route. Cross the farm track, continuing ahead to a stile, beyond which the way is obvious. The stile on to the Morridge road lies just to the right of the crossroads sign.

The view from Morridge extends over the Midland Plain to Wales on a clear day.

Walk south along the road, passing a covered reservoir and a trig point marking the 1,300ft/400m height, the highest point on this route. About 200yds/m beyond the reservoir, turn right, following a track towards Garstones Farm. Where the track swings left, go through a stile ahead, following the wall round, passing through a couple more stiles and a gateway, by-passing the farm. Beyond the gateway, bear right, to a stile mid-way along the bottom boundary. Cross a very narrow field to reach a rough lane. Go right, soon descending steeply to a T-junction. Go right here, then left at Nanscroft, shortly reaching the A523.

Turn right, but in about 50yds/m cross to an unsigned stile by a large hawthorn bush. (There is also a gate into the same field a little further on, if the stile is missed.) Go straight ahead through a gap in the hedge, bearing right across a culverted ditch. Go left to the kissing gate and across the railway line.

This line was built in the early 1900s as part of an effort to open up this remote area and to serve the quarries at Cauldon Low. Passenger services were withdrawn in the 1930s, but freight traffic continued until the 1980's.

Descend beside the concrete post to another kissing gate. Follow the ditch and hedge down to a boggy patch, before the short climb to Revedge. At the top go right on a good track, with views to Shuttlingslow and the Roaches.

Where the track swings left, towards Revedge Farm, follow the broad green lane, which keeps to the right of the farm. Pass through a gate into a field, with a belt of trees ahead. A faint terrace swings to the right, marking the line of the path.

This makes for an obvious gate/stile to the right of the trees. Go over the stile, and follow the path along the edge of the trees, passing Roost Hill

House on the left. Here the path joins a good track. Keep right at the fork. At the junction by the cattle grid, cross the access to Ashenhurst Hall Farm to regain the field path.

Carry on through fields, soon descending to Ashenhurst Mill. Go left crossing the stream on a substantial bridge and climbing to reach a T-junction. Go left, descending again, in a deep cut hollow-way, which soon twists right and then left, where there is a waymarked stile on the right. A narrow path leads through the trees and over a culvert. **This is dangerously overgrown with an unfenced 10ft drop on to brick.**

The path winds up to reach the railway again before descending to fields once more. Follow the left-hand hedge to a stile at the top of the field. Go straight ahead, passing to the right of the large oak to a stile.

Bear right, up to a stile in the top fence. Go right at the finger post, following the route to Lowe Hill. The track soon becomes a tarred lane, passing Lowe Hill Farm before crossing the A523 on a substantial bridge. About 200yds/m further on, the lane swings left.

A footpath following the alignment of the row of cottages on the right marks the line of the old main road, which is joined at this point. About 100yds/m beyond the bend there is a T-junction.

Car drivers who have left their cars at Pikehall Farm should turn right here and go along Mount

Lane for roughly 400yds/m. Bus users should continue straight ahead, down the old road to join the A523 for the walk back into Leek.

31 Longnor, Brund and Fawfieldhead

A stroll out of Longnor leads into the middle Manifold Valley. At Lower Boothlow the walk ascends to Sheen, before visiting Brund Mill. A visit to some of the least known parts of the Staffordshire Moorlands then follows, returning to Longnor over Fawside and Gauledge.

Distance:
9¼ miles/15km
Height gain:
1,140ft/350m
Walking time:
5-5½ hours
Start/Finish:
Longnor Square. Limited roadside and off street parking. The landlord at the Crew and Harpur may allow parking on his car

park, but ask first.
Type of walk:
Little-frequented field paths, some tricky to find. A gently undulating walk.
Public transport:
Longnor has daily bus services from Buxton and Hartington, with less frequent services to Leek. Additional seasonal services.

From the market square, walk east for about 220yds/m. Turn right at the second footpath sign, just past the Cheshire Cheese. Go down through a farmyard, turning left, through a gate. Follow the sign to "Brund via river bank", soon reaching the infant Manifold.

Continue through a series of fields, eventually

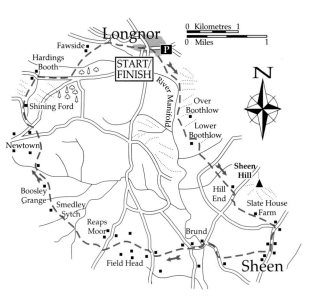

diverging from the river before crossing the track between Waterhouse and Over Boothlow Farms. Bear left, soon approaching Lower Boothlow Farm, where the stile lies to the right of the gates. Go left, passing through the farmyard on to a track. Turn sharp right, descending to cross a small stream, in a valley known as Frog Hole. Follow the track up the south side of Frog Hole.

Sheen Hill comes into view on the left. Cross a cattle grid and, where a lane is reached, go right and then left at the footpath sign. Follow a wall and then the remains of a boundary on the right, to a belt of trees. A deep clough forces the path left, to a bridge. Steps take the path up to a stile, there turning left up more steps before running alongside a wall. Continue by the wall side, until Hill End Farm is reached. Skirt to the right of the buildings, bearing left at a stile to the farm access. Follow the track away from the farm, past the barn, to the road. Turn right.

In 100yds/m, go left at a signpost, heading straight across to reach a gate. A track passes through Slate House Farm yard, onto a tarred lane, passing some holiday cottages. Go down the lane, over the cattle grid, turning left at the junction, rising quite sharply, in a deep cut hollow-way. At the T-junction go right, enter Sheen village, passing St. Luke's church in about 150yds/m. About 200yds/m beyond the church, go right at a stile signed to Brund, bearing left to a stile by an oak tree. Go straight on, following the yellow waymarks, then bearing slightly left. The path soon runs alongside a wall, eventually passing into a fine green lane, descending towards the river at Brund. The lane soon swings right, giving a fine view of Brund hamlet.

At the road, go right for 100yds/m, then left at the footpath sign, heading for the remnant fence, perched on the edge of a short, steep drop to a stream. Descend and cross the stream, to the road, bearing left to Brund Mill. Pass the mill and go over the Manifold. Continue along the lane to a T-junction, going straight ahead, through a stile. Follow the fence up, alongside the course of an old road.

Looking back, Sheen Hill is in view. So is Wetton Hill and the limestone ridge beyond Dovedale, with Carder Low just overtopping the Sheen ridge. The factory is Belle Engineering, who make concrete mixers.

At the end of the field go right, cutting diagonally across to a gate, then following the wall up to the farm. Pass through the farmyard to the road. Go up the lane opposite to Field Head Farm, going right just past the farmhouse, to a small gate in the left-hand corner of the yard. Head to the right of the pigeon lofts to a stile and go straight on, to the far hedge. Head uphill, bearing left of the farm, to the access. Bear left to reach a stile just right of the farm gate. Go straight on, leaving the track to the left. At Knowle Farm, follow the rough path to the right of the barn, passing through a couple of gates, then following the left-hand wall/fence to twin stiles in the wall ahead. Both go into the same green lane, passing a farmhouse on the right.

Go along a broad shallow depression, soon leaving for drier ground alongside, before reaching a road. Go left here, right just before the house and immediately right again, passing a gravestone. Bear left to the wall, following this to the corner, bearing left to a stile. Follow the right-hand fence, to a stile in the field corner, continuing alongside the ditch, fence and wall, to a gate, barn and stile. Carry on a little further to another stile, turning right into a small enclosure. Go left, then right, down a field, to a gate at the bottom. The track crosses the footbridge over Blake Brook, then goes right, following the wall.

Continue by the wall to a signpost. Go left, following the line of thorns, with Smedley Sitch Farm to the left. Bear left at the end of the thorns, heading towards the electricity pole. Go over a slight rise, to the exit stile in the corner of the field. Proceed up to a stile, then bear right to Boosley Grange, reaching a stile just beyond three new trees. Skirt the Grange on the right to a stile, then go left, still skirting the buildings. Descend a little to reach a track, going straight on at a gate.

The track descends through scrub, soon emerging into more open land, where there is a faint path on the right. Follow this down to the stream and pick out a place to cross. Bear left to a bridle-gate and stile. Bear right up the pathless field to Bank House Farm. Go up a track to a gate, following the farm access track to the road.

Go straight down a narrow track, to reach another lane. Turn left, soon reaching a crossroads. Continue down the lane to Shining Ford Farm. Follow the lane uphill from the culverted ford for 150yds/m, going right at a signposted stile. Follow the right-hand wall to the field corner. Head to the right of the pylon, soon crossing a hollow-way and joining a muddy track heading to Hardings Booth Farm. Go through the farmyard to the road, going right and crossing the fine turnpike bridge over the Manifold. Continue along the road for 440yds/m, to a gateway on the left, opposite a clump of trees. Turn left, following a track, making for Fawside Farm, soon crossing the Manifold again.

On reaching Fawside Farm, pass through the farmyard and, where the track goes left, beyond the cattle grid, keep straight on, to a stile. Pass the new planting, going over another stile into fields. Keeping the wall on the right, pass through a couple of fields to a wrought iron gate, there bearing left to a bridge over Hollinsclough Brook. Go straight up the field to the stile at the top, bearing right to the corner, then follow the left-hand wall, passing Gauledge Farm. The path soon joins a lane and enters Longnor village. Go straight on to reach the Square, with its cafe and pubs.

32 Goldsitch and Oakenclough

This walk crosses the main north-south watershed of England twice, visiting the Dane and Upper Manifold valleys, with some tremendous views. Some paths are little-walked and difficult to follow. On some sections you are more likely to see soldiers in full kit than hikers, for these moorlands are regularly used for training. This route avoids the live firing areas!

Distance:
11¼ miles/18km
Height gain:
1,950ft/600m
Walking time:
6-7 hours
Start/Finish:
Royal Cottage bus stop. GR025636. Limited roadside parking on lanes off A53. Alternative

parking at Gradbach car park. GR998662.
Type of walk:
Quiet field paths, some tricky to locate. A lot of road walking but on minor roads.
Public transport:
Royal Cottage has daily bus services from Leek, the Potteries, Buxton and Sheffield.

From Royal Cottage, go down the road signed to Gradbach, with good views ahead to the Dane valley, Back Forest and the telecommunications tower on Sutton Common.

The road passes through a band of contorted rock formations. To the left are Ramshaw Rocks; to the right, Gib Tor.

At the Corner House fork, bear right. In about

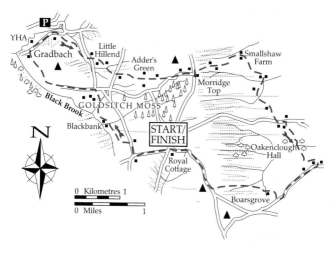

300yds/m, beyond the access to Newstone Farm, go left, alongside a deepening gulley. Where the gulley peters out, bear right to a stile, with Black Brook just to the left.

Black Brook is aptly named, running through soft black shales forming small cliffs.

The path deviates to the left of Blackbank Farm, soon reaching the farm track. Go right, crossing a small bridge, to a T-junction. Right again, then left in 50yds/m, at a signposted stile. Head to the right of Goldsitch House to a stile in the corner. Head for an obvious gateway, but in mid-field, go right, keeping to the left of the shallow depression to reach a stile at the head of the field. Bear left across rough pastureland, passing a standing stone before reaching the road. Go left, along the broad green lane, signed to Gradbach, rising slightly over the southern flank of Gradbach Hill before reaching ruined Cloughhead Farm.

There is a fine view to Roach End and Back Forest as well as down the Dane. Odd rock formations on the right crown Gradbach Hill.

About ³⁄₄mile/1.25km beyond Cloughhead, the track enters a short green lane, then carries on to Gradbach Farm. A waymarked path passes through the farmyard, down a green lane to a T-junction. Go right, soon reaching the hamlet of Gradbach. Follow the lane past the scout camp site and the YHA access, to reach Gradbach car park.

Those parked at Gradbach car park start here.

From the car park continue along the road for 50yds/m, then go right at a signpost by a small gate. An indistinct path leads up to the right to the farm. Turn left, following a wall. Go through a gate, round the wall-end and up a field to another gate. Left here, following the wall to a stile. Continue alongside the wall, then carry straight on to a stile in the field corner. Bear right, making for Bradley Howe Farm. Cross a stream and go over a stile, eventually reaching the road to the right of the farm. Turn right and in about 100yds/m left, up the field to a stile, bearing right on an obvious track.

Follow the track, past a semi-derelict farm, to the road at Little Hillend. Go straight ahead, passing through the gate at the far end of the drive, onto open moorland. Climb steadily, eventually passing through a gap in the ridge near Ann Roach Farm.

Head towards Morridge Top Farm, which is on the skyline. Follow the wall, soon crossing the track to Ann Roach Farm. Go into the field and follow the wall to the corner before turning right and making for Adders Green Farm. Go through the farmyard, to the road, following it up to the A53.

The A53 runs along the main English watershed at this point. Ahead, everything drains to the Trent and the North Sea. Behind, the waters drain to the Dane, the Mersey and the Irish Sea.

At the A53 go left for about 50yds/m to a stile on the right where there is a tremendous view. Bosley Minn and the Cheshire Plain, a view down the Dane valley, and to the north, Axe Edge. East the view stretches across the limestone plateau, to Mam Tor, Rushup and the East Moors. The reef limestone hills at the head of Dovedale can be seen clearly.

Bear right, heading towards Pethills Farm, past the ruined barn, making for the right-hand end of the whitewashed building, to reach a lane. Go right, until the gate into Smallshaw Farm is reached. Go over the ladder stile and head down to the right of the farm. Go over the stile by the farmhouse, turning right, by the fence.

Beyond the ruined cross wall and barn, bear left to a stile in the field corner. Cross the next rough field, then follow the right-hand boundary, soon reaching a stream and then High Ash Farm. Go right, on to the farm track, following this up past Bradshaw. Cross a stream and a cattle grid. About 300yds/m beyond the cattle grid, go left at a stile, following the right-hand fence uphill to a stile at the top, to reach a tarred track.

Go right, along the track, soon reaching the road. Go left, into the dip, there turning right towards Hocker Farm. Where the track bears right to the farm, meander through fields, amply waymarked with splashes of yellow paint on fence posts, telegraph poles and stiles, to reach Oakenclough Hall. Cross the access track and carry straight on, down the walled lane and across Oakenclough Bridge. The path gradually rises through an area of rough pasture, swinging left to reach the brow of the hill. There bear right to a couple of yellow waymarks and the road beside Highfield House.

Turn right, following the road for 1,000m, passing Fair View House and a covered reservoir, almost on top of the hill. The road runs across a wide area of heather moorland, forming the head of Oakenclough. A track on the right leads down to Boarsgrove Farm.

Descend the track to Boarsgrove Farm, unseen from the road. Go through the farmyard, dipping left to cross a stream, then climbing to run alongside a line of trees. At the end of the trees an overgrown track passes on to open moorland. Follow the track left, round the flank of the hill, before passing through a gateway on the right. Follow the ruined wall down to a confluence of streams by a ruined farmstead. Go past the ruin, continuing beside the ruined wall on the right of the stream. There is no path. Progress is suddenly barred by a wall and fence, near another ruined building. Traces of a path go left, down to the stream, where the fence and wall are scaled.

Just beyond the wall, heather moorland begins. The path is supposed to head up the nose of land between the two streams. Initially there is a semblance of a path and some posts as a guide, but soon the route lies through deep, pathless tussock grass. There is 800yds/m of this, on steadily rising ground, until the road is reached, just to the right of the junction. Turn right, along the road.

The land to the left is regularly used by the army for training and there is often live firing. These are the headwaters of the Churnet and there is a view down to Leek, over to the Roaches and Gun, and even to Wales on a clear day.

A further 1¼miles/2km along the road brings the walk to an end, back at Royal Cottage. Car users parked at Gradbach should refer to the start of the text for route instructions from here on.

33 Poolend, Rudyard and Gun

First port of call is Rudyard Lake. The walk then follows the Staffordshire Way to Rushton Spencer. Field paths and ancient roads are followed up on to Gun Moors. A magnificent high level tramp along this ridge ends with a descent to the outskirts of Leek and a return to Poolend.

Distance:
10 miles/16km
Height gain:
1,480ft/455m
Walking time:
5-6 hours
Start/Finish:
Poolend Bridge.
GR966581. No
parking. Car users
should park at
Rudyard, GR955578.
Type of walk:
Contrasting lakeside
paths and little-

frequented moorland
routes. Some fine old
packhorse routes.
Public transport:
Poolend and Rushton
Spencer are both
served by daily buses
from Manchester,
Stockport,
Macclesfield, Leek,
Ashbourne and Derby.
Car users parked at
Rudyard can use the
miniature railway to
reach Rudyard Lake.

From Poolend Toll, at the junction with the Rudyard road, a sketchy path leads down beside the A523 to Poolend Brook. Pass over a footbridge and bear left by a plantation. Go over a stile and carry straight on, across the field to a footbridge. Bear left, making for the left of the large oak. Now bear right, towards the

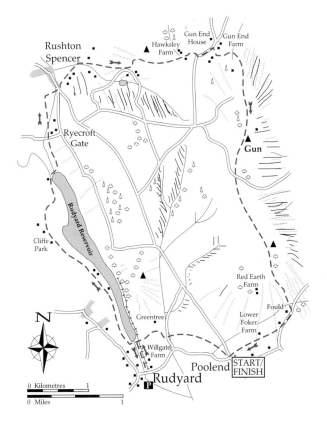

twin-poled pylon. Follow the right-hand hedge, skirting New Grange Farm and passing over the brow of a slight hill, before descending to the road.

Go through the stile opposite, bearing right to a stile on to a lane. Go left, and then right, by the tree stump. Pass through a garden to a stile by a small gate. Follow the left-hand wall, soon topping the rise and reaching a track. Follow the track until it finishes at a stile. Descend by the right-hand fence through woodland to The Dam railway station.

Car users only: To join the walk, either catch the miniature railway from Rudyard car park or walk on the trail from the station, about 500yds/m. To return to Rudyard car park, turn left at The Dam, or catch the train.

All users: Go over the spillway from Rudyard Lake, continuing across the dam wall.

Go straight ahead, following the waymarks for the Staffordshire Way, turning right at the road. Bear left at the fork signed to Cliffe Park station. Left at the next junction, then right at the next. Follow the Staffordshire Way signposts and waymarks, joining a lane, descending towards the lake; then turning north along a good track. The path soon passes Cliffe Park Lodge, a fine derelict building, on the left, then continues through Rea Cliffe Wood, eventually reaching Cliffe Park House. Pass close to the front door of this imposing building. A gate leads back on to a track through fields.

The grounds are partially surrounded by a "ha-ha", which prevented animals getting into the formal garden areas, but gave the impression of there being no boundary when viewed from the house. There is a grand view to the right over the lake to Barnswood and the nearer hills of the Peak.

Descend through parkland, passing a small pond, before veering north-east and reaching the lakeshore, turning left into a lane. Go round the head of the reservoir, crossing the feeder stream and bearing left where the track forks, thus returning to the former railway. Go left, along a path paralleling the vehicular track. After about 1000 yds/m, pass under a road bridge and over the canal feeder. At the next overbridge, go up to the right, over a stile and turn right, passing through a kissing gate, to a bridge. Go up to the canal feeder, then go left to the A523.

Cross the road and go up the lane behind the Royal Oak, passing the school and chapel on the left. Follow the lane for 600yds/m, keeping left at the fork and descending to cross a stream. The rising lane soon reaches a cross-roads. Go right, bearing left in about 100yds/m, going towards the farm. A stile on the right leads into the orchard and through a gate, before skirting round a barn. Bear left up the field heading to the left of the solitary tree.

Make for the stone barn. The exit stile cannot be seen, but lies left of the farm buildings and to the right of the tree. Bear sharply left to a couple more stiles which just clip the corner of the field. Go right, following the fence and passing Heatonhall Farm on the right. Continue until a track is reached, going left here. Heaton lies just to the right. After 150yds/m go right, along a sunken lane.

Pass Toft Hall and swing left to skirt Hawksley Farm, down a deep hollow-way, to cross a stream. The lane climbs, bending right to a road. Go left for about 300yds/m, passing the old chapel on the left, then turn right, along a lane. Pass the tea room on the left then, about 100yds/m from the junction, go left through the waymarked garden gate. Skirt round the back of the house to a waymarked wicket arch, then turn right, alongside the hedge. Descend to a gate, leading to a bridge. Ascend the far bank, through a thicket of holly, passing through a pair of gateposts and bearing left.

Carry straight on, making to the left of the house. The stile is hidden by a large holly bush, just to the left of the gate. Keeping left of Cliff Hollins Farm, pass through the waymarked gateway, bearing left up the field to a stile in the top wall. Turn right along a terrace, which soon finishes. Turn left near a solitary Scots pine, following a ditch and passing Isle Farm on the right. Climb alongside the ditch, soon reaching a stile in the wall. Continue alongside the fence to a gate/stile on the right. Strike across the field, skirting to the right of a clump of gorse. Pass left of the wooden posts around the old bath, and still climbing, soon reach a stile and open moorland. Follow the track up and over the moor to another gate and stile, and go left.

The view northwards stretches over Manchester to the hills beyond Horwich. To the south lies Mow Cop, with its pseudo-castle.

Follow the concrete track upwards, turning right at the footpath sign. A fine high level moorland walk now follows, with extensive views on either side. Pass an area of scrubby woodland consisting of stunted oak, birch and pine, soon reaching the trig point on Gun Hill. Descend south-west along an obvious track, passing an old guidestone.

The tower blocks in the centre of Hanley can be seen in the distance, a reminder of just how close this magnificent countryside is to major urban areas.

At the road go through the bridle gate into a walled lane, where the ridgetop walk continues, the effect somewhat lessened by the belt of beech trees. Beyond the belt of trees the lane ends. Continue ahead, following the right-hand wall. Where the wall kinks right, go straight ahead down the mid-field, to a gate and stile. Bear left to a bridle gate, then follow the right-hand boundary to another bridle gate and into a deep hollow-way. Follow this down to the road.

Go right, passing Fould Farm on the right. Cross a stream, then climb sharply, to Fould Villa Farm, going right, through a stile, then immediately left. Carry straight on to a waymarked stile, left of a holly bush. Straight on, soon reaching a track to the left of Lower Foker Farm. A quick left and right through a gateway leads back into fields. Descend towards the stream, skirting the base of the hill. Pass through the waymarked gateway, bearing left just beyond the ash, over the shoulder of the low hill, to a stile. Follow the right-hand fence, through a tunnel of holly. A waymarked stile leads into a narrow trackway to Poolend Farm. Follow the left-hand wall up to join the A523, close to the bus stop.

Car users parked at Rudyard should refer to the start of the text for instructions from here on.

34 Upper Hulme and The Roaches

An easy walk with superb views. The route follows a grand hollow-way before visiting Tittesworth reservoir and Meerbrook. It then climbs gently to Roach End. A fine high level traverse of The Roaches ridge follows, before describing a graceful arc around Hen Cloud to reach Upper Hulme.

Distance:
7³/₄ miles/13km
Height gain:
1,350ft/415m
Walking time:
5 hours
Start/Finish:
Blackshaw Moor
(Three Horse Shoes)
bus stop. GR009598.
Limited roadside
parking. Alternative
pay/display parking at
Tittesworth reservoir,
GR994604.

Type of walk:
Easy walking on good
tracks or paths.
Optional scrambling
on The Roaches.
Public transport:
Blackshaw Moor has
daily bus services to
Leek, the Potteries,
Buxton, Bakewell and
Sheffield. A seasonal
park and ride service
runs via Blackshaw
Moor.

From the Three Horse Shoes walk north along the A53 to the Churnet bridge, descending the flight of steps at the north-west end. The path soon reaches a stone slab bridge. Cross the stream, going up the field, bearing left to a gate and stile. Follow the wall up past the factory, through the farmyard to the

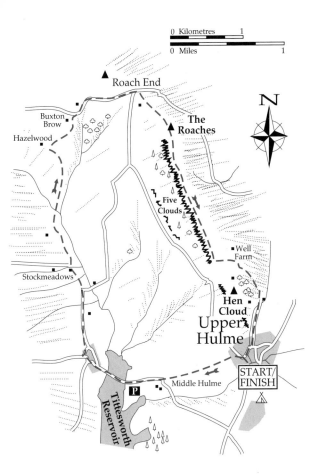

road. Go left, uphill, but in 50yds/m go left, descending a farm access, marked by a large 'np toght of way' sign. Despite the sign, pass through the farmyard, bearing right through two gates to open fields. Go to the end of the field, then go left, following the hedge to a gate and stile on the right. The path runs alongside a deepening "ditch" on the left, the line of an old road.

Gun Hill is in view ahead and there is an odd view of Hen Cloud to the right, where the highest crags just over-top the nearer fields.

Soon the path swings left and crosses the ditch on a single slab of stone, before reaching fields again. Go straight ahead, making for the gate and stile, to a lane. Follow the lane for about 250yds/m, then go through a stile on the right, bearing left to a stile close to the electricity pylon. Go right, along the road, soon passing the entrance to Tittesworth car park and visitor centre.

Car users parked at Tittesworth start here: Cross the northern arm of the reservoir by the bridge.

The reservoir is a popular venue for bird-watchers. The mud flats are the haunt of a wide variety of wildfowl and waders. There is a grand view across the reservoir to The Roaches and Hen Cloud.

Continue into Meerbrook, turning right just past The Lazy Trout. Pass the church, soon reaching Lea Farm on the right. Gun Hill rises to the left. Where the lane swings right, carry straight on along a track, signed to Horse Haylands and Hazelwood, soon passing through Stockmeadows Farm.

About 200yds/m beyond Stockmeadows, bear right at the junction. Continue ahead at the next junction. At the third junction, follow the sign for

Meadows Farm. The track now swings right. Pass to the left of Meadows Farm, through a series of stiles. After the fourth stile, bear left to a gate and stile, heading for Hazelwood House. The path soon diverts to the right at a ditch. Skirt round the edge of the field to a gateway to the right of Hazelwood House. Go right, steeply uphill, with a steep-sided little valley to the right. Continue alongside the fence to a gate, then along the concrete track up to Buxton Brow Farm. Pass through the farmyard, to the lane. Turn right.

There is a good view back to Tittesworth reservoir, extending right down the Churnet to Leek and beyond. Bosley Minn is the prominent rock prow seen to the left of the telecommunications tower.

The lane soon passes through the hamlet of Clough Head, deteriorating thereafter to a green track, which soon reaches the road at Roach End. Cross the road on to the northern end of The Roaches ridge.

This is a very popular part of the National Park. Great efforts are being made to restore the surrounding moorland and this can be helped by keeping to the path. On reaching the ridge there is a sudden panorama to the north and east, taking in Shuttlingslow and Axe Edge, whilst to the right the vista extends to Wales and the Wrekin on a clear day.

Go up the ridge with broadening views on all sides, soon reaching the summit trig point. A broad path runs the whole length of the ridge, with plenty of opportunities for deviation to allow a quick scramble amongst the rocks. The path soon passes

Doxey Pool, a small peaty lake. About 300yds/m beyond the pool, the path descends to the right, through the crags and down to the col between The Roaches and Hen Cloud.

Do not go over the stile leading to Hen Cloud, but locate another, 100yds/m along the same wall. Go across to Well Farm, skirt to the right of the buildings, joining the farm track at a stile just beyond the large ash tree. Follow the track round the base of Hen Cloud, with Ramshaw Rocks rising to the left. Where the track swings to the right, go straight ahead to a stile. Skirt round to the left of a knoll following the path by the stream, along a very muddy path in a narrow valley. Just beyond a duckboarded section, the remains of Dains Mill are reached.

A green track passes between the mill buildings and over the stream, soon reaching the outskirts of Upper Hulme. A concrete track runs steeply down to the ford/bridge in the centre of the village. The main road lies to the left, up the hill. At the A53 turn right for Blackshaw Moor.

(For motorists parked at Tittesworth, there is no need to go to the main road. Instead, turn right at the ford/bridge and go up the lane, passing the factory on the left. Go round the right-hand bend and pick up the described route at the "No Right of Way" sign where a track on the left leaves the road.)

35 The Warslow Square

Beginning with a classic packhorse route from Warslow to Grindon, then along the delightful Hoo Brook to Butterton. A chance then to go "round The Twist" in safety, before crossing Grindon Moor to Onecote. An exercise in route finding then follows to reach Elkstones and find the paths back to Warslow.

Distance:
9¼ miles/15km
Height gain:
1,945ft/600m
Walking time:
5 hours
Start/Finish:
Warslow Post Office.
GR086586. Limited
roadside parking in
village.
Type of walk:
Little-used field paths
and packhorse trails,
some quite tricky to
locate. No serious
climbing.
Public transport:
Warslow is serviced by
Monday to Saturday
buses from Buxton and
Hartington, plus
seasonal Sunday
services. Less frequent
services run to Leek.

From the post office, go down the lane past the church to the main road. Turn left, passing the Leslie Anderson Activity Centre, then go right, down the lane past Pump Farm.

Pass Ivy House Farm and carry on to a signpost, which points to Grindon. The driveway forks and the path goes straight ahead, with the house to the

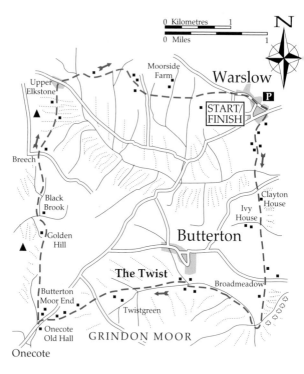

Onecote

left. At the end of the drive, go into fields. Go straight ahead, soon entering a narrow, hedged lane, dipping sharply towards Warslow Brook. At the bottom of the hill, cross the footbridge, go left, then right, up another narrow hollow-way. The track soon levels out as it reaches the road, near to Clayton House Farm.

Go towards the farm, keeping right where the track forks, passing through a gate. After 300yds/m, where the track bears away to the left, go straight on to a bridlegate. Go straight ahead, passing through another gate, then following the left-hand hedge. Cross an unbridged stream, bearing left to a gate at the far side of the field. Bear right here to a stile in the field corner, then follow the fence and hedge on the left.

Much of the Manifold valley is in view. Swainsley Hall can be clearly seen on its knoll above the river.

Pass to the right of Wallacre Farm, crossing the farm access, before continuing south. A couple more gates lead to a road. Continue ahead through a gate, descending into the deep Hoo Brook valley. Pass Broadmeadows Farm, descending through a series of gates and stiles.

At the bottom of the hill go right, along the path sign-posted to Butterton. Cross a small stream, then follow Hoo Brook, in a lovely quiet valley. After 500yds/m, cross the stream by stepping stones. Continue through a series of fields, with the brook on the right. Butterton is soon in view. Near Butterton there is an awkward stile on the right, perilously close to the stream. Cross both with care, bearing left to reach the Brookside area of Butterton. The road bears right and runs along the river! The footway is raised above the road/river on a causeway. Houses line both sides of the road.

Bear left up steps by Brookside Cottage, soon reaching fields. Follow the left-hand wall, but where it kinks left, carry straight on, bearing right at a stile. The next few fields are very narrow with

a constant procession of stiles. Head to the left of
The Twist, squeezing between garden and stream.
Another series of stiles and a stone slab bridge lead
to farm buildings. Head to the right of the barns,
up the centre of the field. The path skirts round the
right-hand side of Twistgreen Farm to reach a
track, which is followed to a road. Go straight
ahead past the National Trust sign, across the ditch
onto Grindon Moor.

*The moor is heather covered and very boggy, a remnant
of what the moors must have been like until agricultural
"improvement" began to make inroads.*

Over the brow of the hill, Onecote comes into view.
Follow the electricity pylons to a track, which soon
becomes a tarred lane. Pass Home Farm, soon
reaching the B5053.

*As this is about the half way point, it is worth knowing
that the pub is about 500yds/m to the left, the only
source of refreshment until Warslow.*

Turn right, and in about 100yds/m bear left to Butterton Moor End Farm, following the track to and
through the farmyard, passing to the right of the
farmhouse. Pass to the right of the barn to a stile
into open fields. Go right to a waymarked stile,
then straight on, into a large field with no obvious
path or exit. Go up the field, keeping on the top of
a low ridge. The exit is marked by a tall post, near a
stile. Follow the right-hand wall/hedge to the end
of the field.

Cross a narrow track to another stile, then resuming

a course beside the fence and ditch. Where these two do a leftward kink, there is a two plank "stile", perched precariously alongside the ditch. Go over both, bearing right to reach a track, following this up to the fence. Follow the fence to a stile in the corner.

Descend into the hidden valley of Blackbrook, soon reaching Blackbrook Farm. Elkstone is signed through the farmyard. Squeeze through a narrow snicket between the barn and farmhouse. An obvious path keeps close to the stream, crossing it to enter rough pasture and scrub. Head in a northerly direction, soon crossing another brook by a bridge. Rough steps lead into overgrown pastureland through which the path wriggles, accompanied by a deep ditch on the left. There are occasional waymark posts and stones.

As the path emerges from the scrub, the wide view north and east to Revidge and Warslow is a revelation.

Go straight ahead to the lane by Breech Farm. Go through the farmyard, passing between the farmhouse and the barns. Round the back is a stile leading into fields. An indistinct path runs alongside a deep ditch, probably an old packhorse route. Keep well up the hillside from the ditch, returning to it to pass through a stile, into a steep field. A grassy track winds down, turning left to cross a stream before reaching Under the Hill Farm.

Keep left of the farmhouse on to a rough lane, following this for about 1,000yds/m, passing Hill House Farm on the left. Descend past Mount Pleasant, soon reaching a junction. Elkstone church lies below to the right. Continue to descend, rounding a right-hand bend to a T-junction. Go right, into Upper Elkstone. Go round a hairpin bend, then turn left along a narrow-walled path between the old school and another building, to reach fields.

Bear left across the field, to a well-hidden bridge in the left-hand corner. Cross this bridge, a stile and another bridge, then proceed right, for a short distance, before turning sharp left. A path zigzags uphill, cutting across the slope of the ground, soon emerging from the wood. Go straight ahead, with the hedge on the right. Pass between the concrete gateposts, heading towards the barn, then bearing away to the right. Go left at a junction of tracks, across open pasture, soon passing through two gates and running alongside a fence. Cross a stream then bear right on an indistinct path, heading towards Moorside Farm. Cross rough pasture, passing to the left of the ruined building. Continue alongside a derelict wall, bearing left along a track to the road. Here go right.

After about 150yds/m, go left at a stile. Pass through a series of fields, crossing a stream near Hoar-stones. The path rises again, passing through a stile before bearing left to a signpost. A flight of steps descends to cross another stream. Pick a way up through gorse to a stile. Follow a line of gorse bushes on the left, passing between a pair of gateposts onto a boggy patch of moorland. On reaching a rough lane, go left, soon passing Water Gap Farm on the right and shortly joining the road on the outskirts of Warslow. Go past the chapel, to the Greyhound and the post office.

Useful telephone numbers

Information Centres
Ashbourne: Market Place. Tel: 01335 343666
Bakewell: Bridge Street. Tel: 01629 813227
Buxton: The Crescent. Tel: 01298 25106
Castleton: Castle Street. Tel: 01433 620679
Edale: Fieldhead. Tel: 01433 670207 (also mountain rescue post)
Leek: Market Place. Tel: 01538 381000
Matlock Bath: The Pavilion. Tel: 01629 55082

Bus and rail information
Available from any of the Tourist Information Centres or from
Buxton: Tel: 01298 23098
Derby: Tel: 01332 292200
Chesterfield: Tel: 01246 250450
Stoke on Trent: Tel 01782 206608

Police
Buxton: Tel: 01298 72100*
Ripley: Tel: 01773 570100
Chesterfield: Tel: 01246 220100
Leek: Tel: 01538 399333*
* These two police stations cover the bulk of the area of this book. The other two cover the eastern fringe of the area.

Acknowledgements

I would like to thank my wife Jane and all those friends who have accompanied me on these walks.

Index

223

Dalesman Walking Guide Series

The Dalesman Walking Guide series is edited by Terry Marsh, one of the country's leading outdoor writers. Each edition is packed with detail given by experts with years of experience of walking the area. This series is aimed at the keen walker who is either familiar with the area or exploring a new walk, and who wants a reliable pocket sized guide with detailed colour maps showing the routes and main features.

NORTH PENNINES
Alan Hall 1-85568-105-6 165mm x 100mm 224 pages £7.99
WHITE PEAK
Martin Smith 1-85568-099-8 165mm x 100mm 224 pages £7.99
CLEVELAND WAY
Martin Collins 1-85568-113-7 165mm x 100mm 128 pages £6.99
SOUTH PENNINES
John Gillham 1-85568-106-4 165mm x 100mm 224 pages £7.99
DARK PEAK
John Gillham 1-85568-100-5 165mm x 100mm 192 pages £7.99
PENNINE WAY
Terry Marsh 1-85568-108-0 165mm x 100mm 192 pages £7.99

To accompany the series:

MOUNTAIN SAFETY

Kevin Walker 1-85568-112-9 165mm x 100mm 256 pages £8.99
A bible for all those who venture outdoors, be it camping, walking or climbing, with detailed advice on subjects ranging from choice of equipment to rope-work, survival and weather conditions, map reading and river crossings. Ideal for individuals as an essential guide for their own safety or as a reference book for group leaders wishing to give instruction on mountain safety.

Dalesman also publishes a successful pub walks series as well as books of shorter walks for families. If you wish to order any of the above books or would like a catalogue showing all Dalesman publications contact: Dalesman Publishing Co Ltd, FREEPOST LA1311, CLAPHAM, Lancaster, LA2 8BR (015242 51225).